DIVIDEND GROWTH INVESTING

GET A STEADY 8% PER YEAR EVEN IN A ZERO
INTEREST RATE WORLD: FEATURING THE 13 BEST
HIGH YIELD STOCKS, REITS, MLPS AND CEFS FOR
RETIREMENT INCOME

FREEMAN PUBLICATIONS

HOW TO GET THE MOST OUT OF THIS BOOK

To help you along your investing journey, we've created a free bonus companion course that includes spreadsheets, bonus video content, and additional resources that will help you get the best possible results. We highly recommend you sign up now to get the most out of this book. You can do that by going to the link below

https://freemanpublications.com/bonus

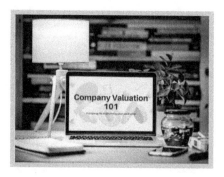

Free bonus #1: Company Valuation 101 video course ($97 value)

In this 8 part video course, you'll discover our process for accurately valuing a company. This will help you determine if a stock is overvalued, correctly valued, or a bargain. Giving you an indicator of whether to buy or not.

Free bonus #2: Guru Portfolios Analyzed ($37 value)

In these videos, we analyze the stock portfolios of Billionaire investors like Warren Buffett. As well as top entrepreneurs like Bill Gates.

Free bonus #3: 2 Stocks to Sell Right Now ($17 value)

These 2 stocks are in danger of plummeting in the next 12 months. They're both popular with retail investors, and one is even in the top 5 most held stocks on Robinhood. Believe us; you don't want to be holding these going into 2021 and beyond.

Free bonus #4: AI Disruptor - The $4 Stock Poised to be the Next Big Thing in Computing ($17 value)

This under the radar company, which less than 1% of investors have heard of, is at the forefront of a breakthrough technology that will change our lives as we know them. Soon this technology will be in every smartphone, tablet and laptop on the planet.

Free bonus #5: Options 101 ($17 Value)

Options don't have to be risky. In fact, they were invented to *reduce* risk. It's no wonder that smart investors like Warren Buffett regularly use options to supplement their long-term portfolio. In this quick start guide, we show you how options work and why they are tools to be utilized rather than feared.

Free bonus #6: The 1 Dividend Stock to Buy and Hold for the Rest of Your Life ($17 Value)

Dividends are the lifeblood of any income investor, and this stock is a cornerstone of any dividend strategy. A true dividend aristocrat with consistent payouts for over 50 years which you'll want to add to your portfolio for sure.

Free bonus #7: Top 3 Growth Stocks for 2021 ($17 Value)

Our 2020 selections outperformed the S&P500 by 154%. Now we've released our 3 top picks for 2021.

All of these bonuses are 100% free, with no strings attached. You don't need to enter any details except your email address.

To get your bonuses go to

https://freemanpublications.com/bonus

CONTENTS

INTRODUCTION

Two thousand five hundred years ago, The Greek Philosopher Heraclitus uttered some of the most profound words in human history.

"The only constant in life is change."

These words ring true in investing as they do in any other field. Back in 1990, you could have retired comfortably with a nest egg of $500,000. All you had to do was invest that money into a Treasury Bill, and you would have earned a steady eight percent every year. That's $40,000 every year from what most experts would consider the world's most stable investment.

These days, if you invest $500,000 into the same Treasury Bill, you won't be getting 8% per year, nowhere near that. In 2020, a Treasury Bill paid just 1.25% every year or $6,250 annually. Six thousand odd dollars barely covers the cost of your utility bills and groceries for the year. Compared to this, $40,000 per year is a princely sum indeed.

The American economy has changed massively over the past 30 years, and the stock market has changed with it. Back in the 90s, the buzzword was growth. The internet was going mainstream, and there were a number of companies that were ready to hit the big time. All that talk of growth fueled the dotcom crash of the early 2000s. Many of the darling names of the late 90s, such as Pets.com, 360Networks and eToys went bankrupt. Many individual investors saw their portfolios wiped out and were left scarred for life by the repercussions of this crash. However, the companies that survived the crash turned themselves into billion- and even trillion-dollar corporations, making their investors wealthy in the process. Meaning all that positivity wasn't totally misplaced.

These days, the talk around the stock market is more subdued. Many people ascertain that asset prices are being fueled by cheap debt, yet cheap debt is necessary because there seems to be no other way to jumpstart economic growth. The previous decade (2010-2019) witnessed the longest ever bull run in the stock market's history, but it's debatable whether economic growth kept up with it. The Coronavirus pandemic brought everyone's fears about another economic crash back to the surface, and the government responded by cutting interest rates even further.

This era is unprecedented. Never in history have governments printed money at such a rate to prop up assets, and never have they slashed interest rates as low as they currently are. This low interest rate environment has hit those who need income from their investments the hardest.

This low interest rate phenomenon is so strong that it has even moved from the real world to the virtual world. The fictional Bank of Nook in Nintendo's best-selling video game *Animal Crossing: New Horizons* slashed interest rates from 0.5% to 0.05%, in an attempt to stimulate players spending on in-game items.

Back in the real world, this low interest rate environment has sparked fears of all manner of scenarios, ranging from deflation to hyperinflation. Which has led to alternative assets such as gold and cryptocurrencies witnessing huge jumps in value. While these assets make the financial headlines, none of this helps an income seeker since these alternative assets don't have any yields in the form of dividends or interest payments.

Speaking of dividends, while government bond yields have plummeted in the past 30 years, stock dividends have largely followed the same path. Figure 1 below illustrates how the dividend yield of the S&P 500 has varied since 1880.

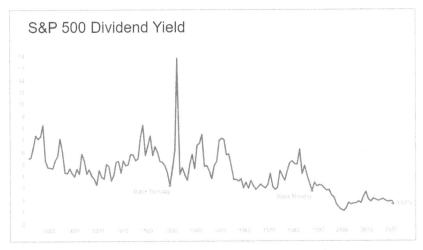

Figure 1: The average dividend yield of an S&P 500 stock

While the general trend of the graph has been downward, notice the massive dip after 1990. While spikes and volatility characterize the large portion of the graph, things have become quite stable recently. Yields have been low, fluctuating between 1 and 3 percent, and it looks like they plan on staying there.

In light of these facts, what should you do if you plan to live off the income from your investments?

SEARCHING FOR YIELDS

Most investors have had one of two reactions to declining yields. The first has been to withdraw their initial investment (known as the principal) from the markets and stick the money in a savings account. The reasoning is that if the stock market doesn't provide yields, then it makes no sense to expose money to market risk. The problem is that the average savings or money market account doesn't pay investors anything.

As of this writing in October 2020, Wells Fargo's Way2Save account pays a pitiful 0.01% interest. That's not a typo. It really is $1/100^{th}$ of 1 percent. They ought to call it Way2Deplete for all the good that interest rate does. Investors who choose this option avoid stock market risk, but they lose money once you take inflation into account.

The second reaction has been to sell stocks to generate income. For example, if you were earning five percent yields on your portfolio but are now earning just one percent, you could sell enough stock to generate the equivalent of that missing four percent yield.

There's only one problem with this approach. If the stock market falls, you'll have to sell more stock to cover that yield gap. When the stock market is high, you won't need to sell as much, however you'll have less to sell in the first place.

This seems to be a Catch-22 for income investors. Fortunately, that's where we come in. Our objective in this book is to help you spot those investment opportunities that can bring you a high yield without the additional risk that accompanies most high yield stocks and funds.

There are still great income-generating stocks out there. Our view is you need to think outside the box a little bit to spot them. The media and Wall Street are focused completely on the likes of Facebook and Amazon. They have all but ignored the companies we're going to highlight in this book. It's not as if these income-generating companies are small either. Many of the companies we're about to highlight have market caps greater than 30 billion dollars.

This is where the opportunity lies for you. There are companies out there that are steadily paying their shareholders monthly and quarterly paychecks, with yields greater than five percent, and in some cases as much as 10 percent annually. In today's zero interest rate environment, a yield of five percent and above is high. Combined with capital gains, you're you're looking at returns above eight percent per year from the stocks we will discuss.

The first part of this book will focus on how we've arrived in such a low interest rate environment. Then we'll move to the factors we focus on for profitable long term income investing. Finally we'll spotlight specific stocks, REITs, MLPs, ETFs and funds which satisfy our income investing criteria.

It doesn't matter what the size of your portfolio is now. You don't need a special investing account either, all you need is a standard brokerage account or a retirement account. The companies and strategies we're going to highlight will help you generate a full time passive income and supercharge your retirement. We'll also show you how you can grow a small account to a much larger one thanks to the power of compounding and dividend reinvestment.

All it takes for you to realize this potential is a little work and dedication. Put in the work today, and you and your family will benefit tomorrow.

1

WHAT HAPPENED TO SAVINGS ACCOUNTS AND BOND YIELDS?

"You used to have income and safety. Today, with treasury yields at 0%, you have income or safety."

— HOWARD MARKS, CO-FOUNDER, OAKTREE
CAPITAL MANAGEMENT.

Before we dive into the best income generation opportunities in the stock market, it's important to understand the economic conditions which led us to this point. After all, bank savings accounts and certificates of deposit (CDs) used to be the norm in everyone's savings plan. These days, they don't provide value, as much as take it away from you when you factor in inflation. So what happened to the savings account, and why do we find ourselves in this position today?

Back in 1981, the average three-month CD paid investors 18.3%. Don't get too excited; the interest rate was this high because inflation was equally high. As time wore on, inflation decreased, and so did bank interest rates.

In the 2000s, the interest rate on a CD was between three and five percent, which was still two percentage points higher than inflation. Then came the real estate and stock market crash of 2007-2009. As bad as the stock market crash of 1930 was, it isn't far-fetched to say that the global financial crisis of 2007-2009 had a similar generational impact in the following decade.

This is because the global financial crisis was the first time that one of the pillars of the American economy, real estate, had crashed. Before 2008, real estate has gone just one way, up. No one could have imagined an America where real estate would be worth less tomorrow than it was worth today. Real estate accounted for a large portion of American wealth, and once it dropped, people's savings and access to credit dropped as well.

As a result, the economy suffered, and the government had to figure out ways to solve the crisis. One option was to let everything fall following the principles of the free market. This option would mean assets (stocks and real estate) would drop to record low levels, and after that, market forces would figure out the way forward. In real world terms, this would be equivalent to digging a hole and continuing to dig until you reached the other side.

Most economists agreed that letting assets plummet to rock bottom prices was a terrible idea, with uncertain recovery times and further negative consequences beyond just a bad economy. The specter of the Great Depression also hung heavy on the government's head. The prospect of mass unemployment was unbearable, and as a result, the government choose a second option.

MONETARY BAND-AIDS

The Band-Aid that the government applied was modest at first. In 2008, the US Treasury Department, led by former Goldman Sachs CEO Henry Paulson, announced that the government would guarantee bad assets in the most troubled banks. This was to avoid an all-out collapse of the financial system. This program slowly expanded to securing assets even at good banks. Followed by selectively stepping in to rescue banks close to the government's heart, while letting the others die (*Why the Fed saved AIG and not Lehman*, 2008).

Banks borrowed $700 billion from a government program named the Troubled Asset Relief Program (TARP), headed by former Goldman Sachs VP Neel Kashkari. With the governments now guaranteeing the bank's bad assets, these banks soon returned to making a profit.

However, a larger problem brewed. All these newly guaranteed assets needed to be paid for. So now the question was, just *who* was going to pay for all of this? Enter the Federal Reserve bank, headed by Ben Bernanke. The Fed began buying these terrible assets en masse.

So how did the Fed pay for this? It's simple, they started "printing money". Not literally, that's the US Treasury's job, but by purchasing Government securities the Fed adds money to its own balance sheet and newly created dollars to the balance sheets of banks such as Wells Fargo and Goldman Sachs.

Banks then get more money in reserve to lend to consumers, while avoiding a potential run on the bank from people wanting to withdraw their money. In return, the Fed takes ownership of assets, primarily Government bonds.

Economists greeted this level of money printing with great alarm. It wasn't the first time a central bank had tried this strategy. The Weimar Republic of Germany had tried it in the mid 1920s. Their policies led to massive hyperinflation, which threw the country into economic and social turmoil, ultimately leading to the political rise of Adolf Hitler. So to say the Weimar experiment didn't work is like saying the Hindenburg flight didn't go to plan or that Abraham Lincoln didn't enjoy his evening at the theater.

However, cloaked by the fancy name of "Quantitative Easing" (QE), Bernanke's Fed printed so much money that it became the norm to do so. The UK followed, as did the European Central Bank. The Swiss followed shortly thereafter. Meanwhile, the Japanese merely laughed and said that they had been doing this on and off since the 90s and were masters at it, despite the results showing otherwise. (*Japan's Expansionist Policies Have Brought Unexpected Results*, 2019).

Imbalances

While QE may have benefitted banks and larger institutions, there wasn't much of a trickle down effect for the middle or working class. Small businesses rushed to the bank when they learned big companies were being bailed out, only to find that they had to fulfill ridiculous terms such as having a million dollars in revenue and ten years' worth of profitable account statements. In short, the businesses who could borrow money were the ones who arguably needed it the least.

In the name of reducing asset risk and non-performing loans on their books, banks denied money to the engine room of the economy. Small businesses went bust and wages reduced. Economic reports didn't highlight this because unemployment wasn't increasing. Wage decreases are different from unemployment. Former investment bankers became bank tellers, former business owners worked hourly jobs, and former skilled technicians began waiting tables. So strictly speaking, people were still employed, even if they were in much lower paid positions than before.

The stock market, which is composed of huge companies, did very well with QE. The government purchased bonds from commercial banks, mainly in the form of US treasury notes. This led to bond yields plummeting and stock prices becoming more attractive in comparison to bonds. This led to a flood of money going into the stock market, which is why we see companies like Apple and Amazon now with a market cap of over 1 trillion dollars.

This is the essence of the "K" shaped recovery that economists have been talking about recently (Chen, 2020). The K economy has been highlighted recently as a reaction to the Coronavirus pandemic, but it is part of a larger phenomenon that started after the global financial crisis. From June 2008 to October 2020 (the time of writing), the Fed added almost $4 trillion into the money supply through QE.

A roaring stock market has the bonus side effect of being a political bargaining tool. It's easier to point to rising stock prices and claim to be a genius. But that doesn't change the fact that to print money cheaply, interest rates need to be cut.

This is why rates are at rock bottom today. Because of this low interest rate policy, we have seen rates on Savings and CD accounts plummet to below inflation. Whether the approach is misguided or not is debatable. However, there's no denying the aftereffects of it.

Negative Mortgages and Other Financial Quirks

It's easy to sit back and rail against the government for bad monetary policy. It's equally easy to frame an "us versus them" style argument and say that the rich are greedy, immoral, and so on. The fact is that a lot of the thinking behind QE was backed by solid economic theses. The primary thesis behind low interest rates and flushing the economy with cash is to get people spending money.

The thought process runs like this. With cash readily available for banks, they increase lending to ordinary folks. These people then use the money to buy goods and services that benefit small businesses. As small business prospects grow, so too does the economy and eventually, the government can stop printing money.

The problem is that everything went pear-shaped somewhere along the way. Banks didn't lend money to the people that needed it the most because they had to satisfy the government's strict leverage rules and set aside additional money for potential losses. The government's intention with this rule was to avoid a repeat of the credit crisis where the banks needed bailing out. As a result, cash didn't trickle to the underprivileged players quickly enough while the financial institutions gobbled it up in hoards.

This meant governments around the world printed even more money, then needed creative solutions to get people to spend more. One method was to then cut interest rates to a level where there was zero incentive to save. This is not just an American phenomenon either, The UK's rates currently sit at 0.1%. Switzerland and Denmark are at -0.75% and -0.6% respectively. Japan, who pioneered QE, sits at -0.1%.

The negative signs aren't a misprint. The government in these countries will charge borrowers money for holding onto their cash. This is why the Swiss giant

UBS decided to charge people who held more than 500,000 EUR in savings accounts. Denmark even offers negative interest rate mortgages, which have decreasing payments over time. The effects of these creative policies are still unknown. However, in the States, we can make some ready observations for what QE's economic effects have been thus far.

First, the predicted economic boom from increased spending never came. People lost far too much to begin spending money once again immediately. After all, financial crises don't just bring monetary hardship, they also affect our psyche.

If you're reading this book, you likely have a parent or grandparent who grew up in the aftermath of the Great Depression. This was an entire generation brought up lacking faith in both economic institutions and their own future. This led to characteristics such as frugality with money, and a penchant for savings versus spending. It was only after World War 2, 16 years after the Great Depression when Americans really started spending again.

We're seeing similar effects now as a result of the Global Financial Crisis. At the beginning of 2010, Americans had around $4.8 trillion in total savings across all institutions. In August 2020 that number was $11.5 trillion. If you look at the data since 1975, savings rates have roughly doubled every ten years, regardless of the interest rate environment, but in the last ten years, they have nearly tripled.

Second, one of the underlying economic theories that supported QE was an old friend of any undergrad Economics student, the Phillips Curve. The Phillips Curve theory states that as economic spending increases, inflation increases. As this happens, the economy grows and more job opportunities are available. This leads to lower unemployment. However, between 2008 and 2020, this didn't happen. Inflation remained low, and many people just exchanged higher-paying jobs for lower-paying ones.

This year, the Fed's current Chairman, Jerome Powell, finally said out loud what everyone was thinking all the time. The Phillips Curve was dead. He was correct, but around 60 years too late in saying it. In fact if you look at the data, inflation and unemployment haven't been correlated at all at any point since the 1960s.

The early 1960s was a low unemployment, low inflation environment. The late 1960s was a low unemployment, high inflation environment. The 1970s was a high unemployment, high inflation environment. Between 2008 and 2013 we had high unemployment, low inflation and between 2013 and 2018 we experienced a low unemployment, low inflation environment.

In 2020, we are in an environment where inflation could potentially increase, and unemployment would increase because of it. After all, as more money is printed, the greater the spending amongst those who can access it. This drives prices up. Meanwhile, nationwide shutdowns are forcing more businesses to either lay off staff or permanently close their doors, which leads to an increase in unemployment. Welcome to the K-shaped world.

Meanwhile in the Stock Market...

Nowhere is the evidence of the K-shaped world more stark than with the stock and real estate markets. There aren't any real-time trackers of real estate prices, so media interest has been subdued there. However, America is experiencing a real estate boom (D. Williams, 2020). Many real estate experts are scratching their heads at the way the market is behaving. How does one explain record-high house prices against high unemployment numbers?

The stock market has been even more nonsensical. It began from the bottom of 2009 when QE fueled its growth. Until 2015 or 2016, everyone was under the impression that QE was working and that the economy was recovering. However, with the passing of five years since the crisis, it became increasingly obvious that QE wasn't having its intended effect.

Famed Value investor and hedge fund manager extraordinaire Seth Klarman wrote to his investors in 2015 that the stock market was about to enter a bear market (*2015 Letter - Klarman tells investors he is looking for bargains amid "stealth bear market,"* 2015). Klarman's analysis was correct. Things stopped making sense. However, even an investor of his caliber misjudged the effect of the K-shaped recovery.

Klarman's prediction was correct when looking at the broad market. Since 2015-2016, the Russell 2000 index, which tracks small cap companies, has been flat, with periods of intense volatility. In contrast, the S&P 500 has risen like a phoenix, conquering one all-time high after another and scarcely losing breath. What's going on here?

It turns out that the more privileged of the privileged few have used QE to astonishing effect. The S&P 500 is heavily weighted towards the so-called FAANG-M stocks. These companies are Facebook, Amazon, Apple, Netflix, Google, and Microsoft. You see, as QE was unfolding and as everyone was coming to grips with the 2008 financial crisis, the internet finally stepped up and delivered what it had promised back in the late 90s.

Increasing technological advances by these companies, coupled with cheap money, meant growth was inevitable. As these companies grew, their weight in the S&P 500 grew as well. The index has historically sought to maintain equal weighting between all 500 components. Today, FAANG-M accounts for an astonishing 25% of the index, and drives the majority of the growth. (*Trade Signals - FANG Stocks Up 400%, S&P 500 Index ex-FANGs up 35%, S&P 500 Index up 45% (2015-Present)*, 2020).

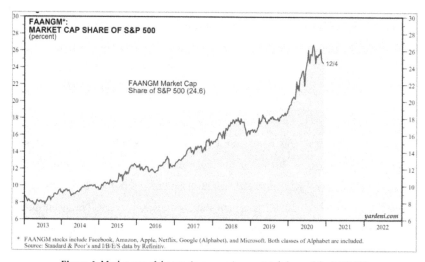

Figure 2: Market cap of the top six companies as a total share of the S&P 500

Figure 3: The relative performance of the S&P 500 if you remove the FAANG-M stocks

This means if you buy an ETF that tracks the S&P 500 (like SPY or VOO), you're essentially buying exposure towards FAANG-M. This is great if you're chasing capital gains. However, an income investor is left out in the cold. Of these six stocks, just Apple and Microsoft pay dividends. Even then, Apple had to be cajoled and threatened by activist investors before it agreed to pay. These companies operate in rapidly changing industries, and it's unfair to expect them to pay stable dividends.

The performance of the stock market in 2020 further highlights how heavily weighted the market is towards these companies. Here is the performance of these stocks as of November 26th 2020 (YTD):

- Facebook: 34%
- Apple: 58%
- Amazon: 72%
- Netflix: 50%
- Alphabet (Google): 32%
- Microsoft: 35%

While these six companies have soared, if you subtract them from the index, the rest of the S&P 500 has remained relatively flat. Right now, the stock market is in a weird place. Everyone acknowledges that there is something resembling a bubble going on. However, no one thinks that a pop is justified. After all, these huge tech companies are performing incredibly.

In fact, they're doing so well that any company with even a whiff of tech about it gets sent to dizzying heights, which is another indicator of a bubble. For example, Tesla is now the 7th largest company in the world by market capitalization, passing Warren Buffett's Berkshire Hathaway. Elon Musk's company joined the S&P 500 on December 21st 2020, which will likely see the index growth concentrated in even fewer stocks.

The Tesla halo has passed to companies such as Nikola and other unproven, zero-revenue (yes revenue, not income) companies such as Hyllion, which have hit billion-dollar valuations.

Other companies such as Zoom and Peloton are still selling for absurd earnings multiples, but there's seemingly no end in sight. The pandemic was supposed to erase these gains and pop the bubble, but the market roared right back within a couple of months. To say that the market is in a weird space right now understates what's going on. No one can make any sense of things, and perhaps this is a good thing for an income investor like you.

THEN VERSUS NOW

The primary takeaway from this economic lesson/horror story is that change happens all the time, and there isn't anything you can do to predict it. It's easy to connect the dots in hindsight, but when you're in the thick of a situation, it's close to impossible.

Instead of focusing on what you could have or should have done, it's best to reorient your focus towards what you can do. The second half of this book will cover principles and give you examples of companies that can generate both income and capital gains for your portfolio.

To illustrate how much the world has changed, let's look at how your income streams look now versus in the past. First, let's take the case of a standard savings account with $100,000 deposited into it. Here are some of the other assumptions we've made:

- Inflation is set at three percent per year over a 20-year period
- Column 1 is the year
- Columns 2 and 3 contrast growth in an account that pays one percent interest (more representative of the current landscape) with an account that pays five percent interest (more representative of the 1980s/1990s)
- The value in each column is what your money is worth after accounting for inflation.

Year	1%	5%
1	$97,115.38	$100,961.54
2	$94,313.98	$101,932.32
3	$91,593.38	$102,912.44
4	$88,951.27	$103,901.98
5	$86,385.36	$104,901.04
6	$83,893.48	$105,909.71
7	$81,473.48	$106,928.07
8	$79,123.28	$107,956.22
9	$76,840.88	$108,994.26
10	$74,624.31	$110,042.28
11	$72,471.69	$111,100.38
12	$70,381.16	$112,168.66
13	$68,350.93	$113,247.20
14	$66,379.27	$114,336.12
15	$64,464.48	$115,435.50
16	$62,604.93	$116,545.46
17	$60,799.02	$117,666.09
18	$59,045.20	$118,797.49
19	$57,341.98	$119,939.78
20	$55,687.88	$121,093.04

You can see the effect that the one percent "depletion" account has. Because of inflation, you're steadily losing money as the years go by.

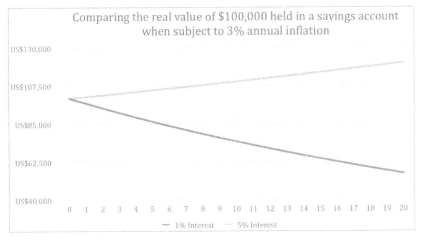

Figure 4: The above table visualized

In real terms, you'll end up with half of your original principal after 20 years. Meanwhile, your five percent interest bearing account increases the value of your money and creates true wealth.

Let's now look at how bond returns change depending on the coupon you're paid. Here are the assumptions we've made when creating the table below:

- Your initial investment principal is $500,000
- The withdrawal rate is four percent. This is how much you'll withdraw every year to pay for expenses.
- We've contrasted the returns between a bond that pays 3.5% and another that pays 0.01%.
- The second column lists the principal left over after withdrawal when the bond pays 3.5%. The last column lists the leftover principal when the bond pays 0.01%.

- You will withdraw four percent of the number that is listed under the "3.5%" and "0.01%" columns every year.
- To keep things simple, in this example, we have listed the nominal values, which are not adjusted for inflation

Year	Principal	3.50%	0.01%	Principal
1	$500,000.00	$517,500.00	$500,050.00	$500,000.00
2	$497,596.15	$515,012.02	$480,865.39	$480,817.31
3	$495,203.86	$512,536.00	$462,416.80	$462,370.57
4	$492,823.08	$510,071.88	$444,676.01	$444,631.54
5	$490,453.74	$507,619.62	$427,615.84	$427,573.08
6	$488,095.78	$505,179.14	$411,210.19	$411,169.08
7	$485,749.17	$502,750.39	$395,433.96	$395,394.42
8	$483,413.84	$500,333.32	$380,262.98	$380,224.96
9	$481,089.73	$497,927.87	$365,674.04	$365,637.48
10	$478,776.80	$495,533.99	$351,644.82	$351,609.66
11	$476,474.99	$493,151.61	$338,153.83	$338,120.02
12	$474,184.24	$490,780.69	$325,180.43	$325,147.91
13	$471,904.51	$488,421.17	$312,704.76	$312,673.49
14	$469,635.74	$486,072.99	$300,707.72	$300,677.65
15	$467,377.88	$483,736.10	$289,170.95	$289,142.04
16	$465,130.87	$481,410.45	$278,076.80	$278,048.99
17	$462,894.66	$479,095.97	$267,408.27	$267,381.53
18	$460,669.21	$476,792.63	$257,149.05	$257,123.34
19	$458,454.45	$474,500.36	$247,283.43	$247,258.70
20	$456,250.34	$472,219.10	$237,796.31	$237,772.53

As you can see, a four percent withdrawal rate reduces your principal in both cases. This is understandable since you're withdrawing more than what you earn in interest. However, when you earn 3.5% your principal reduces to $456,250 compared to $237,772 in the 0.01% interest case.

Another way of interpreting these results is to say that you'll lose more than half your money to withdrawals over 20 years in the latter case, whereas you'll lose less than 10% in the former scenario.

This highlights the importance of focusing on the returns your investments are making if you plan to withdraw part of the principal to live off. Remember that this table doesn't even account for inflation, so in real terms your money is worth even less in the 0.01% scenario.

You will always have to combat inflation, and your portfolio needs to overcome these drags on performance.

Which is why from now on, we will emphasize finding investment opportunities that give you a combination of capital gains and dividends. It isn't enough to focus on just one of them since this will lead to your principal being depleted and lowering the amount you can withdraw, as the above two tables show.

It's not just enough to consider inflation, though. We also need to consider the costs associated with investing. Which is precisely what we'll do in the next chapter.

FREEMAN INCOME INVESTING RULE #1

AN IDEAL DIVIDEND PORTFOLIO STRIKES A BALANCE BETWEEN INCOME AND CAPITAL GAINS

2

ONE PERCENT MATTERS – WHY YOUR FINANCIAL ADVISOR MAY BE KILLING YOUR RETIREMENT

The first place most prospective retirees head to when they have issues with their portfolio is a financial advisor or a financial advisory company. Like most individual investors, financial advisors have been battered since the 2008 crisis. This is because of how the financial advisory industry is set up. Most managers distinguish themselves on the basis of outperformance. The greater someone outperforms the broad market, the more sought-after they are.

This might sound a lot like how hedge funds work, but there's a crucial difference. Hedge funds have the freedom to invest in whichever assets they like and use any strategy that they please. It's entirely between the fund manager and the investors. If the fund manager decides to use astrology to predict markets, the manager is free to do so if investors like the idea.

Financial advisors don't have near as much leeway when advising clients. They need to deal with largely unsophisticated clients who need to be guided away from risky investments. The advisor has to prioritize capital preservation above all else, which means they can't take risks like hedge fund managers do. Furthermore, they need to make clients money without putting it at risk of a drawdown since this will lead to their clients walking out on them.

A drawdown is defined as a loss in account equity. Let's say you invested $100,000 in the market, and the value of your portfolio decreased to $50,000. That's a 50% drawdown. If you decide to sell the stocks in your portfolio, it becomes a realized loss. If you hang onto it, it's unrealized and isn't a cash loss. The problem for financial advisors is that most clients are impatient and this impatience turns unrealized losses into fully realized ones. This damages the reputation of the advisor, and as a result, they stick to promoting staple investment sources.

However, this brings another issue with it. The recommendations that they hand out and the strategies they ask their clients to follow come across as being plain vanilla. If your advisor is telling you to buy the same thing that a popular financial magazine is, what's the need to pay the high advisor fees? The financial advice industry has come up with a creative way to sidestep this issue.

FUND RECOMMENDATIONS AND COMMISSIONS

Visit many financial advisors, and the first thing many of them will tell you is to divide your portfolio into a 60/40 split between stocks and bonds. If you're an income-seeking investor, the split will be the other way around, with 60 percent allocated to bonds and 40 percent to stocks. Some advisors still recommend subtracting your age from 100 and using that allocation for stocks. So if you're 60 years old, you'll allocate 40% to stocks and the rest to bonds.

This method of portfolio allocation makes no sense. It was originally proposed as a shortcut and an excellent way to get started thinking about portfolio allocation as you grow older. It wasn't meant to become a rule. Proper portfolio allocation is all about your goals and the level of risk you're willing to bear.

Financial advisors will then recommend specific mutual funds and other investment products to you. Herein lies another problem because if your advisor works for or is affiliated with a large investment firm, they'll almost certainly push one brand of mutual fund and investment choices to you. This is because in addition to charging you advisory fees, the advisor earns commissions from those mutual fund houses. This isn't to say that they're pushing bad mutual funds at you. It's just that you're only given a choice of a tiny subset of all the investment products that are out there.

Most people go to advisors because they are intimidated or overwhelmed by the variety of choices, so they blindly accept what their advisor tells them. By pushing seemingly specialized mutual funds, advisors sidestep the question of why their strategies seem pretty basic. They'll respond that most basic strategies tend to be poorly executed and that the fund they're recommending executes it the best.

They're not wrong in saying that it can be tough to execute basic strategies in the market. However, the notion that one mutual fund does it better than another is extremely hard to prove. When you buy a mutual fund, you're buying a specific set of investment objectives. These objectives can either be growth or income-oriented. There are many subdivisions to these categories depending on the types of instruments the fund invests in.

No matter the strategy, the average mutual fund aims for outperformance. They measure their performance against a market-relevant benchmark. For example, a mutual fund that aims to generate tax-free income will invest in municipal bonds, private tax-free bond issues, and treasury inflation protected securities (TIPS). They'll measure their performance against the muni bond index. If the index rises by five percent and the fund rises by six percent, that's outperformance. Similarly, fund managers will choose appropriate indexes when investing in stocks. If they're investing in European small cap companies, they'll benchmark themselves against the European small cap index.

There are two issues with this approach. Let's take a look at them.

ISSUE ONE - CONCENTRATION AND
DI"WORSE"IFICATION

The first issue from concentrating on particular asset classes is that fund managers hamstring themselves. They don't do this by choice, of course. Many complicated laws are surrounding how a mutual fund manager should structure their funds. Most of them set up their funds with the aim of gaining pension fund money. Pension funds have hundreds of billions of assets under management and need to allocate that money somewhere.

They do this by splitting that giant hoard of cash across different asset classes. The specific asset classes will vary from one fund to another, but the average pension fund manager will never stick all of their money into a single asset class. If that asset class fails or underperforms, it'll result in billions of dollars of unrealized losses. Besides, pension fund managers have their own benchmarks to worry about.

From a mutual fund manager's perspective, the best way of increasing the assets they manage is to hyper specialize in an asset class. This is why certain mutual funds invest solely in European small cap healthcare stocks and nothing else. If they receive allocations from pension funds, it's a windfall for the fund house and the fund manager.

The problem occurs when your financial advisor recommends funds like these to you. They'll push these funds to you in the name of diversification. However, you likely don't have billions of dollars in your portfolio. If you invest in European small cap healthcare companies, your portfolio is extremely concentrated. You need to invest in European large cap stocks as well. What about bonds? Well, invest in European bonds as well. All of these are foreign holdings, you'll need American exposure as well. You'll buy American large cap, small cap , and mid cap mutual funds. You'll buy bond funds, real estate funds, and who knows what else. By the time you're done diversifying your portfolio, you'll hold around seven to eight mutual funds and will have spread your money so thin that none of these instruments will have any effect on your portfolio.

This is what the famous mutual fund manager Peter Lynch described as di"worse"ification (Lynch & Rothchild, 2000). Lynch helmed Fidelity's Magellan fund from 1977 to 1990 and earned an average annual return of 29.2% for his investors. It's safe to say he knows what he's talking about.

At the end of the year, the fund manager and your financial advisor will point to their benchmarks and note that they outperformed the market. This justifies their collection of fees from you. We'll get to fees shortly and highlight their effect on your portfolio. After you pay fees, your portfolio that's spread too thin will be in a worse position than what it started the year with. Since no single instrument in your portfolio will affect the total portfolio's value, you'll end up going backward after fees and inflation.

ISSUE TWO – THE PROBLEM OF OUTPERFORMANCE

Performance in a mutual fund is measured against a benchmark, not the overall market. Unless the fund aims to invest in the entire market, you're unlikely to find it benchmarking itself against the S&P 500 or other major market indexes. By being too broad in their investment approach, they can't attract pension fund money.

We mentioned that by hyper specializing, fund managers hamstring themselves. The reason is that it's hard to make money when your investment options are limited. Consider the case of our European small cap healthcare fund. How many companies can it possibly invest in? There aren't many profitable small cap companies to invest in, to begin with, let alone profitable small caps situated solely in Europe. Once you add the healthcare requirement, your world of opportunities shrinks massively.

There's also the problem of portfolio concentration. This issue was highlighted first by Peter Lynch in his book *One Up on Wall Street*. Let's say a fund manager is running a portfolio where three companies are doing well, and three aren't doing so well. There are no other companies in their portfolio. As the three companies' market value rises, and the value of the three underperformers falls, the weight of the high achievers increases in the portfolio. Much like how FAANG-M has taken over the S&P 500, these three will dominate the fund manager's portfolio.

If the mutual fund manager was an individual investor, the logical step would be to dump the three underperformers and invest more money into the outperformers. However, we're dealing with the money management industry here, so nothing is logical. The fund manager will be rapped on the knuckles by their pension fund investor, who'll ask them about their increasing concentration risk. As a result, the mutual fund manager will sell their profitable holdings and buy more underperformers to redistribute portfolio weights.

This creates a ton of trading activity since rebalancing is a daily task for a mutual fund. This generates trading commissions from the fund's prime broker, and those fees are passed on to you. At the end of the year, the fund outperforms its benchmark, and everyone pats themselves on the back.

Except, who's to say that the benchmark is a valid measure of outperformance? What if the S&P 500 gains 30% and the European small cap healthcare index gains just 10%? That's gross underperformance. Even if the fund gained 15%, on the year, it underperformed the broad market by 50%! That's not anyone's idea of success.

Most mutual funds fail to outperform the broad market (Pisani, 2019). Instead of specializing deeply in obscure healthcare stocks, the manager would have made more money by merely buying everything in the S&P 500 and sitting tight. However, that's too simple, and they won't earn fees by doing that. Neither can your financial advisor justify their fees by recommending such a simple strategy.

This is why most mutual funds are a dud when it comes to investing for growth or for income. Last year, the S&P found that after ten years, 85% of large-cap funds underperformed the S&P 500, and after fifteen years, nearly 92% trailed the index.

The fund benchmarks make no sense, and they aren't even targeted to benefit small investors. They're targeted at big pension funds that have to distribute their assets across multiple classes to achieve an adequate level of diversification. If you replicate their asset allocations, you'll spread your money too thin and will end up trailing the market.

FEES

All of the previous issues occur before we even get to the biggest problem with mutual funds. The fees are exorbitant. The numbers themselves don't seem too high, but when you account for them against the average performance you can expect, things don't look rosy. Mutual funds (except index funds) charge 1 to 1.5% in annual fees. That's 1.5% of your principal, not gains. If you invested $100,000 in a fund, you'll pay $1,500 every year no matter what the market does.

There are other fees as well. The most notorious of them all is the load fee. Loading is the process by which a mutual fund incorporates your money into the rest of its portfolio. A fund will charge fixed loading fees. If you're charged fees on deposit, it's called a front loading fee. If you're charged on withdrawals, that's a back loading or withdrawal or redemption fee. Whatever the name is, you'll have to pay to access your money.

Then there are 12B-1 fees that go towards paying for the advertising and marketing expenses. In essence, you're paying the manager to advertise the fund to even more pension fund managers and pay for any additional office space or bonuses they might need.

These days, mutual fund managers are conscious of how unfair their fee structures can be and have reduced fees by a large amount. There are no-load funds and funds that don't charge 12-B1 fees. However, some funds offset this by charging a greater percentage of assets as performance fees. At the very least, no mutual fund will ever decrease its performance fee.

Let's run some numbers now and look at how just a performance fee of one percent affects your profitability on an initial investment of $100,000.

We'll compare this to a broad market ETF like the Vanguard 500 Index Fund ETF (VOO) that charges just 0.03% of principal as fees. We'll assume that both funds return seven percent every year and that inflation is two percent.

Year	1% Performance Fee	0.03% Performance Fee
1	$103,883.50	$104,871.12
2	$107,917.81	$109,979.51
3	$112,108.79	$115,336.74
4	$116,462.53	$120,954.93
5	$120,985.34	$126,846.78
6	$125,683.80	$133,025.64
7	$130,564.73	$139,505.47
8	$135,635.20	$146,300.94
9	$140,902.59	$153,427.43
10	$146,374.54	$160,901.06
11	$152,058.98	$168,738.74
12	$157,964.19	$176,958.20
13	$164,098.72	$185,578.04
14	$170,471.48	$194,617.76
15	$177,091.74	$204,097.82
16	$183,969.08	$214,039.66
17	$191,113.52	$224,465.78
18	$198,535.40	$235,399.77
19	$206,245.51	$246,866.37
20	$214,255.05	$258,891.52

At the end of 20 years, you'll have $214,255 after accounting for inflation and one percent portfolio management fees. This is a 3.88% compounded annual growth rate (CAGR). On the other hand, you'll have $258,891 after 20 years if you pay just 0.03% performance fees. That's a CAGR of 4.87%. In absolute terms, you'll make 20% more over 20 years. Fees alone account for this difference since everything else was the same.

Where can you find investment funds that charge you just 0.03% per year? Well, that's what index funds and index ETFs are for. Funds issued by Vanguard charge just 0.03% management fees every year. What's more, index funds are more likely to earn the seven percent return that we assumed in this calculator. This is because they simply track the S&P 500, which usually returns this much over the long run. In fact, the index has returned an average of 8% per year since 1957 (Maverick, 2019), and as we've already seen, most mutual funds underperform the index.

This level of underperformance doesn't matter to your financial advisor. They'll get paid no matter what. What's more, they'll even earn money based on the number of funds they can push to clients. Fund houses pay them handsome commissions, and this puts many financial advisors in conflict with your best interests.

This isn't to say that all financial advisors are bad. Many of them are fantastic and truly have their clients best interests at heart. It's just that you need to be aware of what the investment advisory industry is like and act accordingly. You are more than capable of constructing a portfolio that generates steady income all by yourself. As we'll show you in this book, it isn't as hard as you think it is.

FREEMAN INCOME INVESTING RULE #2

ALWAYS UNDERSTAND THE FEE STRUCTURE BEFORE WORKING WITH A FINANCIAL ADVISOR

A QUICK WORD ON ANNUITIES

As times have turned more uncertain, many investors have been pushed towards annuities by their financial advisors. Annuities are an insurance product, and they can get pretty complicated once you begin to dive into them. The basic premise of every annuity is the same. You invest a certain amount of cash with a life insurance company or annuity provider. Then tell them when you wish to start receiving monthly payments. From that date they'll pay you that fixed sum every month until you pass.

Unlike mutual funds, there's much good to be said about annuities. They provide guaranteed cash flow, and this is what many investors are seeking in retirement. However, the biggest knock against them is that they don't account for inflation. Your fixed payments will be eaten up over time if inflation rises. For example, if you want to earn $10,000 per month for the rest of your life, starting ten years from today, you'll have to invest roughly $2.3 million.

Assuming you live for another 25-30 years, a monthly guaranteed income of $10,000 is going to help you live a good life even if inflation rises by two to three percent every year. However, the catch is that you need $2.3 million in the first place, and this is a pretty large sum that not everyone will have.

Our objective in this section is to help you understand how annuities need to be evaluated. The reason is that many financial advisors will push them to you as a wonderful investment tool. They do this because they earn a ton of commissions by selling them. On average, insurance companies pay advisors three to four percent of the invested amount as commission.

On top of this, some features of an annuity can work against you if you're not careful.

Term

There are two aspects to an annuity's term that you should be aware of. The first is the date from which you wish to start receiving monthly payments. For example, the further in the future this date is, the higher your monthly payment will be. It's also tied to your age. The older you are when payments begin, the higher the payments will be.

The second aspect of the term of the annuity term is how long you want your payments to last. You can opt for a fixed term (say ten years), as well as payments until the end of your life, or payments till the end of your spouse's life. Once the term ends, the remaining principal may or may not be refunded, depending on your choice.

If you choose to have the remaining principal refunded, you'll receive a lower monthly payment. There are also many other moving parts to an annuity than the term, so it's best to consult a life insurance specialist to determine how much you can expect to receive. Also, your chosen location and residence matters.

Inflation

Inflation is the biggest negative of opting for an annuity. Since your monthly payments are fixed, you'll receive less cash in real terms as time goes on. This doesn't always have to be a negative. If you've provided enough for your dependents and opt for payments beginning when you're 70 or older, you won't necessarily have to worry about inflation. At that age, income generation matters the most, and an annuity can give you that security.

However, if you're younger, an annuity will put the brakes on capital growth and will actually lose you money. It's equivalent to letting cash sit in the bank instead of putting it to work. This is why an annuity isn't a sure-shot solution to income generation issues. The closer you are to the conceivable end of your life, the more an annuity makes sense. You also need to consider how much you would like to leave your heirs after your passing. If maximizing their inheritance is your highest priority, then an annuity won't do you much good.

FREEMAN INCOME INVESTING RULE #3

**THE ONLY "GUARANTEE"
WITH ANNUITIES IS THAT THEY WILL
EVENTUALLY SUCCUMB TO INFLATION.**

Company Risk

Annuities are products of insurance companies, and as with every insurance contract, counterparty risk is real. For example, you can take the right step and insure your home for flood insurance. However, if the insurer (your counter-party) cannot pay, your insurance contract is worthless. This is pretty much what happened during the financial crisis in 2008. Many banks had insurance contracts on their portfolio of bad assets. However, the insurers weren't able to pay and, as a result, a few banks went under.

There is a possibility that the insurance company responsible for your annuity might go bust. Insurance companies go out of business all the time. You can mitigate this risk by opting for a large insurer, but the risk remains.

Although many states in the U.S. have Departments of Insurance that regulate against this, whereby if an insurer goes bankrupt, the annuity contracts are assigned to other carriers, effectively guaranteeing the contract. It's important to know if that is the case in your state of Residence.

Annuities aren't fully FDIC-insured. You might be able to recover a few pennies on the dollar of your investment, but there's no way you will ever be adequately compensated. We're not saying annuities are unsafe. It's just that trusting your entire nest egg to an annuity is not a good move. It leaves you exposed to counterparty risk, no matter how large the counterparty is.

Remember that there are deep mechanisms that govern which product is recommended to you. Complexity is never a sign of competence.

Now we've covered what to watch out for, let's focus on something more positive, how you can implement a profitable income investing strategy.

3

THE IDEAL INCOME INVESTING STRATEGY

I f the investment advisory business isn't going to do you any favors, what kind of investment strategy should you follow? The answer to this question isn't as hard as it seems. The financial markets provide you with comprehensive tools and instruments to design a portfolio that generates your desired income level. Before we get into the portfolio, though, it's important to take some time to look at the overall strategy you need to adopt.

Successful investing isn't a question of merely picking the right stocks and then letting the income roll in. Many investors fail to fully take advantage of market conditions because they aren't temperamentally suited to maintaining a long-term income-generating portfolio. They aren't entirely to blame for this because surprisingly little investment advice caters to long-term wealth generation.

Even respected magazines and media outlets parrot a few lines about investing for the long term but turn resolutely back to focusing on short-term market forces. They report daily market movements as if they have a significant impact on your portfolio. This tricks investors into thinking that they need to jump in and out of the market to take advantage of every tick up and avoid every tick down. While this sounds good in theory, it's impossible to pull it off in practice.

This is just one of the many behavioral changes you need to make. Your investment strategy isn't so much about picking the right stocks as much as it's about helping you get out of your way when it comes to making money.

INVEST FOR THE LONG TERM

Your investment timeline is the best place to begin. How long do you think you need to remain invested to generate profitable returns? Let's look at an example. Let's assume you had the chance to invest in a company; let's call it General Widgets Corp (GWC).

GWC rises by 3,000% over the next two years, but it seems to be overheated. Let's say you sell it and capture a 3,000% gain. Over the next two years, your decision appears vindicated because GWC loses more than 90% of its previous gains. Your decision to time your entry and exit made you an increase of 3,000% in this stock over four years. That's an excellent performance no matter which way you slice it.

However, there's an issue with this approach. You see, this isn't a made-up example that we've highlighted. GWC is Amazon, and between 1997 and 1999, the company's stock rose 3,000% and then lost 90% between 1999 and 2001.

If you mapped the performance of Amazon's stock from 1997 to 2017, the stock has risen by more than 30,000%. What if you had simply bought Amazon and held it, without bothering about what the market was going to do over the short term? You would have netted a 30,000% gain by this time. Suddenly, earning 3,000% over four years doesn't seem too attractive, does it?

Long-term investment is what works best in the markets. Curiously, most long-term investing is defined by a *lack* of activity. On a portfolio level, long-term investors might be active. For example, Warren Buffett isn't a passive investor by any means. He constantly looks at Berkshire Hathaway's portfolio and buys new companies or sells existing holdings.

However, at a position level, he's pretty much inactive. This is why he's held Coca-Cola since 1988 (and made 1,750% in the process, combined with more than $7 Billion in dividend payments). Plus, Buffett has maintained many of his insurance holdings since the 1970s.

Good things take time to grow, and it makes no sense for him or you to attempt timing the market's short-term fluctuations. Predicting the short term is tough, and this is where many investors go wrong.

Short-Term Market Moves

The trouble with figuring out and anticipating short-term market moves is that there's no sensible and repeatable way to predict them. There's no telling what might move the markets on a day-to-day basis. What's more, your margin of error when predicting short-term market moves is a lot less. You need to be more precise with your predictions since there isn't much room for you to be wrong. For example, if you've bought a stock for $100 and plan on selling it within a year, your expected profit isn't going to be too large.

Assuming it moves in step with the market's long-term growth rate, you can expect it to increase by 10%. This equals a final price of $110. If you sell it for $105, which is just $5 away from the maximum price of $110, you've given up 50% of your potential profit. What if the price dips to $90 before it reaches $110? You're planning on holding onto it for just a year, so how can you be sure that the price will rise to that level again within your time frame?

Stock prices rise by a lot more over the long term, giving you the luxury of being less accurate and still profiting by a large amount. Looking at the example of Amazon that we highlighted, a short-term investor who bought the stock in 1997 and sold it in 2000 would have seen most of their gains erased. A long-term investor who bought it in 1997 and simply held on for 20 years would have earned far more. If Amazon stock fell by a few points in a short-term bear move in 2017, it would hardly impact their 30,000% gain.

Long-Term Market Moves

The great thing about long-term market moves is that they always track fundamental factors. For example, if you had the chance to buy Disney stock in 1995, would you have bought it? A cursory glance at the company would have told you that it had valuable intellectual property, a licensing business like no other, and a strong brand that everyone was familiar with. There are very few people on earth who haven't heard of Mickey Mouse, Donald Duck, or Elsa from Frozen. It was a good bet that the company would be around for many years to come.

We're not saying that investment analysis should be reduced to a few lines such as this. However, as far as starting points go, this is a pretty good place to begin. You are investing in a strong company that has many things going for it, is more likely to work out than an investment in a small company that no one has heard of. Disney has weathered more storms and has seen more ups and downs.

Similarly, what if you had the chance to invest in Coca-Cola back in 1983? You would have probably jumped on it without hesitation. Here is the point we're trying to make. Coca-Cola's stock sank after the 1987 market crash, and Disney underwent major restructuring to address its falling stock in 2003 and 2004. Short-term investors would have bailed on the stock during these lows and would have tried to jump back in once things became good once again. However, how does one know when things have turned good?

In the long term, a business's stock price will reflect its earnings growth. Amazon's stock rose and fell many times during its meteoric rise. However, when viewed from 1997 to today, its stock price has grown in proportion to the company's fortunes. It's far easier to invest for the long term since you'll have to deal with real numbers and business prospects.

You don't have to worry about what the economy does or what the monthly jobs report number looks like. You simply buy and hold on until your investment thesis is no longer valid. You sell only when your original reason for investing isn't valid anymore or if you want to use the cash. You'll sleep better at night and won't have to worry about what tomorrow will bring.

Another advantage of long-term investing is that you don't need too many great ideas to succeed. If you had withdrawn your money from Amazon after the 3,000% gain in 1999, you would have had to reinvest it somewhere. Finding investment opportunities isn't an easy task. It's not as if great ideas grow on trees. They don't come by very often, and if you're someone who has a full-time job, it's going to be pretty tough to find new opportunities.

With long-term investing, all you need are a handful of good ideas, and you're set for life. After all, you aren't looking to sell your holdings anytime soon, and your money grows by itself without you having to do anything with it. It's easier to come up with two or three great investment ideas over the course of a decade than it is to come up with them every three months.

What To Ignore

Focusing on long-term investing means you ignore short-term market moves as well as the media hysteria that accompanies them. The financial media exists to sell views and clicks, and the sophistication with which they present data is a veneer. The media's job is to gain enough eyeballs so that advertisers can pay them more. Don't mistake round the clock news coverage for intelligent analysis.

It's a lot like a person who responds to work emails at three in the morning. Very few good decisions get made at that time of the day, and odds are that nothing real or informative is achieved by responding to work emails at that hour. The media often trots out experts who recommend stocks. There are even shows dedicated to buying and selling stocks with literal bells and whistles to drive the point home (we're looking at you, Jim Cramer).

All that these shows do is emphasize the need to trade over the short term. In this sense, the financial media is a lot like the nightly local news. How many times have you heard headlines like "A deadly killer in your area… tonight at nine"? More often than not, these headlines are just baiting you into watching the news. Do you remember what the local news reported a year ago? Probably not. Treat the financial media with the same degree of importance.

Brokers and certain media houses give priority to covering Wall Street analyst reports. These reports are useful if you want to learn the broad brushstrokes of a company's business. If you need to know in-depth information about a company's various business units and how its departments operate, an analyst's report is a good resource.

However, Wall Street, by its very nature, is a short-term beast. When these reports talk about buy/sell ratings and earnings projections, they focus on quarterly performance. The concept of figuring out what a business will be worth in ten years is alien to these people. This is because the majority of Wall Street clientele are hedge funds and pension funds. Hedge funds mostly love trading over the short term, and pension funds need these reports to determine whether there's any asset allocation risk to their portfolios over the short term.

Every Wall Street analyst knows who they're creating reports for. If they started focusing on long-term projections, their employers would lose the millions in fees that hedge funds and pension funds pay them. The average retail investor, such as, yourself cannot pay this amount of money to justify such coverage. This is why you need to take analyst coverage with large heaps of salt. Use the reports to gain high level knowledge of companies, but don't use them to figure out valuations or even sentiment.

This is why we recommend that you remain invested for a period of at least five years, with ten or fifteen years being ideal. Focus on the business's quality, not just on the dividends it pays or how fast its stock rises. The quality of the company comes first. This is what creates wealth. Stock markets don't rise linearly, so ignore short-term market moves. This includes any pandemic-induced bear markets or election-related volatility.

MINIMIZING RISK

What is risk when it comes to investing? The simple definition is that risk is the probability of you losing your entire investment. The less you know about what you're investing in, the more you risk losing your investment.

Many Wall Street analysts like to equate risk with return, but this is a fallacy. Common investment advice suggests that high risk equals high returns. However, this isn't true. Risky assets often appear to yield high returns because this is what convinces people to invest in them. For example, if someone asked you to invest in a gold mine in a war-torn country, your first instinct would be to ask for something that would make this risk worthwhile. Typically, this compensation is a high rate of return.

However, does the high rate of return reduce your risk? Not really. Your chances of losing money are just as high no matter what the return is. It isn't as if some rebel warlord is going to look at your high rate of return and call off a coup. Divorce risk from return, and you'll begin to evaluate risk in much better ways.

This is especially true in today's low-yield environment. Many assets are being pushed to investors, such as yourself, with the promise of generating high returns. The returns that these assets generate are not correlated to their risk profiles. If it were that easy to evaluate risk, everyone would construct mathematically precise portfolios all the time.

The best way to get a handle on risk is to ask yourself an acceptable level of personal risk. Everyone views risk differently. You might look at that gold mine and run away from it, but someone else might be willing to stomach the loss of the money invested in it. As an income investor, your definition of risk is pretty easy to narrow down. You're looking for assets that will generate cash flow regularly. This means these assets should be predictable, or as predictable as possible.

Volatility

In the stock market, there's a word for measuring predictability. It's called volatility. The more an asset price jumps around, the more volatile it is. Think of it this way. Let's say you're running a business and employ two people. Both of them are excellent workers and deliver outstanding results. However, they have different personalities.

The first person is a steady and reliable worker. He arrives on time, every time, and diligently carries out all of the tasks he is assigned. If you were to grade his work on a scale from 1 to 10, his output would be a 7, a highly predictable 7. It's good enough for you to make money in the business, even if it lacks the brilliance of a genius.

The second employee has the potential to give you results that are 10 out of 10. She has a real talent for their work and possess a streak of brilliance that the other employee doesn't have. However, she is more "erratic." You never know *when* she will deliver said results, even if the results may be brilliant when you get them. Imposing hard deadlines doesn't work with her, and she might not even show up to work for a few days. Despite all this, when she does deliver her work, it's always exceptional.

Clearly, the second employee is going to give you more sleepless nights. Thanks to her brilliance, she could take your business far, but it's going to be bumpy. She might even let you down a few times, even if she manages to pull something out of a hat in the end. The first person is a relatively dull but steady earner. Your business isn't going to make the headlines for creativity, but you'll chug along at a good pace. The question is: Which person should you choose to keep if you had to keep just one?

Clearly, this depends on your outlook and goals for your business. If you're someone who wants to achieve the highest growth possible and produce the best possible products, the second employee is the one for the job regardless of the potential struggles. If stability is your goal and you don't mind missing out on your business's highest goals, the first is the person for the job. Is this analogy sinking in yet?

The first employee represents a steady company that produces predictable cash flow and doesn't throw too many surprises in investing. The second company is a hot growth stock that is always in the news, has a ton of attention, and is expensive to buy. It jumps around all the time and is volatile. However, it could give huge capital gains by the time it grows. Tesla is an example of such a company, while Coca-Cola is an example of the former.

From an income investor's perspective, stability is all-important. This means you need to minimize volatility. You need an asset that is going to show up to work at nine every day, is going to give you a predictable work output, and is going to behave in ways you can handle. Above all else, it should not possess any artistic streak that may or may not go anywhere. You can hold such stocks in your portfolio, but their weight needs to be minimized.

Beta

The easiest way to measure the volatility of a stock is beta (β). Beta is a measure of volatility, and it's often substituted as a measure of risk. We'd like to reiterate that volatility does not equal risk. It equals risk only for someone looking for steady income without significant drawdowns.

The overall market index is pegged with a value of one. A beta value greater than one indicates a stock that is more volatile than the market average. A beta value that is less than this indicates a stock that is less volatile than the market. If steady income without a massive upside is your main goal, low beta stocks are the kind you should prioritize owning. Your goals should be to earn decent gains (not the highest) with as much stability as possible.

To demonstrate this, here are some five year Beta values for a handful of popular companies as of November 26th 2020 (source: Yahoo Finance)

- Nio – 2.61
- Tesla – 1.97
- Apple – 1.35
- Amazon – 1.3
- Chevron – 1.26
- Kinder Morgan – 0.93
- AbbVie – 0.69
- AT&T – 0.67
- Pfizer – 0.64
- Coca-Cola – 0.55
- Wal-Mart – 0.52

As you can see, the hot growth stocks which don't pay dividends tend to have higher beta values, whereas the steady income generators have lower beta values.

SEEK TO LIVE OFF GAINS, NOT WITHDRAWALS

A popular piece of retirement advice is the four percent withdrawal rule. If you've read anything about retirement planning, you've probably read of this. The idea is to withdraw four percent of your nest egg every year to have money to pay for expenses. There's a lot of misinformation about this, so let's explore it in more detail.

William Bengen is the person we have to thank for this rule. Bengen is a retired financial advisor who proposed that a withdrawal rate of four percent is a good rule of thumb to begin figuring out how much a person needs to withdraw to ensure their portfolio provides for them in retirement.

Bengen's conclusion was based on data gathered between 1926 and 1976. During these periods, a million dollar portfolio composed of 50% stocks and bonds would not have depleted in less than 33 years if four percent of it was withdrawn every year. This means you could have withdrawn $40,000 every year safely. Bengen intended to begin a discussion on safe withdrawal rates, but it turned into something else entirely. Instead of being the beginning, it became the end of all conversations regarding withdrawal rates.

There are many problems with assuming a four percent withdrawal rate. The first is that if the market crashes early on, the amount of money equivalent to four percent will be very low. Living expenses don't fluctuate with the market, and people will end up selling more of their portfolio to pay for their living costs. This is exactly what happened to people who retired in 2007 and saw their portfolios crash within 12 months.

By withdrawing too much (in percentage terms), they took money off the table precisely when they ought to have been loading up even more. As a result, they couldn't fully partake in the bull market that occurred over the following decade.

Another point to note is that retirement spending isn't flat. The early years of your retirement will account for larger expenses. This is often due to people still providing for their children and supporting them financially. Data from the Bureau of Labor Statistics supports this. According to its Consumer Expenditure Survey, the mean spending for households headed by 55 to 64-year-olds was $65,000 in 2017. Spending dropped to $55,000 between ages 65 and 74, and after age 74, it fell to $42,000. Housing costs remained steady for older people, and health care expenses increased, but nearly every other category, including transportation, entertainment, clothing, food and drink, declined sharply.

This is why reducing your withdrawal to a fixed amount every year, and limiting yourself isn't a good idea. It's also why we mentioned previously that it's best to seek income and capital gains in some proportion. If your portfolio earned an average of eight percent every year, and if your portfolio was worth one million dollars, you could safely withdraw $80,000 without touching the principal.

This method isn't foolproof, of course, since no one can predict how the markets will behave. However, it's better than adopting the four percent rule. That rule works if your nest egg is large and if your living expenses are comparably low. It isn't a solution that works for everybody.

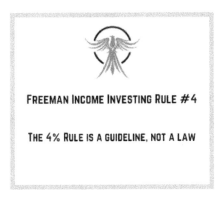

FREEMAN INCOME INVESTING RULE #4

THE 4% RULE IS A GUIDELINE, NOT A LAW

CUT OUT THE MIDDLEMEN

The investment advisory industry lives off commissions. Everyone has the best investing strategies that they'll charge you an arm and a leg for. Once you're done paying commissions, your gains are typically worse than the market average. Get off this treadmill if you want to make real money.

Commissions are a big reason for this. We've already illustrated a scenario where commissions and fees eat into the majority of your gains. These days, brokerage commissions are zero or pretty close to it, whether you choose an app-based broker or a regular one. One step above this is the fees that fund managers charge. Minimize this with low cost ETFs and index funds instead of opting for fancy mutual funds that rarely outperform the market.

To make our point even more precise, paying one percent of your assets as fees is unjustified. Instead, stick to funds that charge less than 1% every year. The only exceptions are the closed end bond funds (CEFs) we'll be discussing later in this book. Minimize your trading activity and choose discount brokers who charge zero commissions. The easiest way to make money is to stop losing it. Think of the following example when you evaluate prospective fund investments.

Let's say you're filling a bucket with water, but this bucket has a large hole at the bottom. The amount of water you'll need to pour into the bucket needs to overcome the water that drains at the bottom. That hole at the bottom is how fees behave when it comes to investment performance. You can't eliminate the hole when investing in funds, so it's important to minimize it as much as possible.

4

DIVIDENDS 101

Dividends are a staple of every income investor's portfolio. Many novice investors chase dividends and yields but very few actually understand what dividends are and how they work. This chapter aims to help clarify many of the myths and poor investment practices that dividends have created amongst investors. Many of them succumb to greed and end up investing in the wrong companies.

The dividends we're talking about here refer to cash dividends, not stock dividends. Stock dividends or bonus shares are great, but they don't produce income for you. Investors often view a cash dividend as the surest sign of a company's stability. However, it's not as simple as this.

The presence of a dividend is an excellent thing, but basing your entire investment thesis on it is not the smart thing to do. After all, even a failing company can pay a dividend to cloak poor performance. Sadly, many investors fall for this trick regularly. Instead of looking at the dividend, you need to look at the quality of the business first and foremost because the better a business is, the more sustainable its dividend.

Remember that your aim is to earn steady returns (capital gains and income) over a period of at least ten years. This is why it's imperative for you to look at the business and the quality of its cash flows instead of merely the dividend it pays you. With this point being made, let's look at why it's a good idea to invest in dividend-paying assets.

WHY DIVIDENDS ARE A GOOD INVESTMENT INDICATOR

Let's say you have two companies, A and B. Both companies earn a steady 12% on equity every year and post similar revenue growth. The difference is that A pays 20% of its earnings as dividends to its shareholders while B doesn't. What can we infer from this example?

For starters, we can quickly surmise that A offers its shareholders more benefits. Not only is it giving its shareholders capital gains (unrealized), it's also providing its investors with realized gains in the form of a dividend. The 20% of its earnings that it pays its shareholders are real gains investors earn in their portfolios.

Stability

If A pays dividends, it means that its management has enough cash set aside to take care of business for the next year at the very least. They have enough money to cover their current liabilities and other expenses. What's more, they've also budgeted for capital expenditures and have reinvested enough money to ensure the business is competitive.

This probably means that the environment they're facing isn't all that competitive. If you knew tough times were ahead, or if you knew that you lived in a dangerous environment, would you ever distribute your resources to others? You'd probably hang onto them no matter what. Cash is a company's most important resource. If there are dark clouds on the horizon, a company isn't going to distribute its cash.

Business is always competitive, and if a company is sure that it can withstand challenges, it often means that it has a dominant share of the market. The bigger and more entrenched a company is, the more it can afford to distribute to its shareholders and still maintain its competitive edge.

Sharing company profits with shareholders is also an indicator of a management team recognizing how best to utilize cash. Holding onto cash for no reason is wasteful. After all, if the company can't use it to enhance its competitiveness or acquire other companies, the cash is better off in their shareholders' hands. The cash distribution also creates an expectation in the minds of the shareholders. The market begins to expect the company to maintain its stability and its dividend.

This means management needs to plan ahead of time and maintain a business's competitive edge. There is a disadvantage here in that a company cannot take huge risks or gambles. If their business targets disruption, they might not react quickly enough to address new challenges. However, generally speaking, dividends force management to think deeply about investing capital and bringing returns to shareholders.

All of this means company A is a much better investment than B from an income-generation perspective. B has a few advantages because it can reinvest more of its cash to ward off any disruptive threats. Take the example of Amazon and Google. Despite being huge in their industries, both of these companies regularly face threats to their business models. If a person sitting in his or her garage invents a better search engine algorithm than Google's existing algorithm, Google's entire business is threatened. They need cash in the bank to buy their competition and protect their business.

Similarly, Amazon's eCommerce business model is based on offering the lowest prices. The company underprices its products to kill competition and gain market share wherever it goes. It needs cash to maintain profitability and to fund its acquisitions. Both of these companies could land in hot water if they went around distributing cash to their shareholders.

The only tech giants that pay dividends are Microsoft and Apple. Even these companies pay a very small portion of their earnings to shareholders. Apple currently pays 24% of its income while Microsoft pays 35% (Sparks, 2020). Both are on the lower end of the scale when it comes to dividend-paying stocks. Technology is an inherently unstable line of business where disruption is a constant threat.

As an income investor, your priority is to seek stability. Dividends point to this factor in a business quite reliably.

Performance

Stable companies that pay dividends don't appreciate as much as non-dividend-paying companies do. The very fact that these companies pay a portion of their profits out to investors means their ultimate growth is capped. However, a more significant reason is that most of these companies are simply too big to grow larger. Take the case of Coca-Cola or PepsiCo, two competitors which both happen to be stellar dividend-paying companies.

How much larger can they grow? Unless Elon Musk delivers on his promise to colonize Mars by next year, it's hard to envision these companies growing their businesses by even ten percent every year. However, this lack of growth doesn't mean their stocks don't perform well. This is because dividend-paying stocks become a safe haven during both bull and bear markets. They tend to fall less than their non-dividend-paying counterparts. The presence of a dividend acts as an assurance that things aren't as bad with these companies as they could potentially be with others.

JP Morgan Asset Management (JPMAM) conducted a study in 2013 that looked at US dividend-paying stocks' investment performance versus those that don't pay dividends (*US dividends for the long term*, 2013). The study tracked companies from 1972 to 2010 (38 years) through all the ups and downs during that time. JPMAM found that companies that paid and raised their dividend payouts returned an average of 9.5% per year over this time period. In contrast, non-dividend-paying companies returned just 1.6% over the same time.

We must point out that increasing dividend payments was a large factor in the 9.5% yearly performance. An increasing dividend means company profits were probably growing over this time period. However, don't confuse a dividend increase with revenue increases. Often, companies will maintain their dividend to preserve stock price levels.

A good case of this was Boeing in 2020. The company has had a terrible decade and faces lawsuits worldwide thanks to faults in its 737 Max jet. On top of this, its 747 airliner finally became obsolete and was retired without a clear replacement. These events, along with declining defense industry contracts, led to a CEO's resignation and a huge turnaround plan being initiated. Then came COVID-19.

With plane orders hitting rock bottom, Boeing declared a loss for the year 2019 and projects to make a loss in 2020 as well. However, its dividend is stable. Management figured preserving the dividend would help the stock price remain at decent levels. Withdrawing a dividend is often viewed as heretical by the institutional money management industry. As a result, many managers maintain dividends, even when the company is losing money.

This is why it's crucial to assess a business's quality instead of merely looking at its dividend. In Boeing's case, the company is large and dominant enough to plausibly bounce back. It has just one competitor in the commercial airplane manufacturing industry because of the considerable competitive advantage (also known as a "moat", as popularized by Warren Buffett) caused by the immense amount of capital needed to manufacture planes. Boeing management's decisions to preserve the dividend might prove to be a good one in the long run. Our point isn't to say that you should buy Boeing. It's just that you need to take all factors into account. A business is much more than its dividend.

As the JPMAM study shows, the presence of a growing dividend is a good starting point from which you can narrow down good candidates that will provide you with a steady cash flow for the long term.

YIELDS AND PAYOUT RATIOS

Two metrics that are often quoted when looking at dividends are the yield and payout ratio. The **yield** is calculated by dividing the annual dividend amount by the current price. If a company paid two dollars in dividends and is selling for $100, it's yielding two percent. The tricky thing with yield is that it is always based on the previous year's payout amount.

For example, let's say a company paid two dollars the previous year, but its stock price is currently selling for $10, having fallen from $100. It hasn't paid a dividend this year, so its yield will be 20%. Many new dividend-focused investors chase high yields thinking they're sustainable when in fact, they aren't. A falling stock price usually creates a high yield.

The key to successful dividend investing is finding a company with a high yielding stock but pays out a sustainable portion of its income. That's what the **payout ratio** measures. It's calculated by dividing the dividend payment by the net income and is expressed as a percentage. In the previous section, we highlighted how Apple pays just 24% of its net income to shareholders. This means Apple's payout ratio is 24%. Low payout ratios combined with high yields are an investor's dream. However, the market typically ensures that such combinations don't remain in place for very long. As more people notice the situation, investors jump into the stock, and the price rises, which causes yields to fall.

At the time of writing (late 2020), the average S&P 500 dividend yield is less than two percent. Anything above five percent is considered high yield for an individual stock. REITs or real estate investment trusts yield higher than five percent regularly, but that's because of the way they're structured. They're legally obliged to pay 90% of their profits back to shareholders, which automatically boosts their dividend payments. We'll examine REITs in more detail later in the book.

When looking at payout ratios, it's essential that you pay attention to the ratio between the dividend payment and free cash flow as well. Free cash flow is calculated by subtracting capital expenditures from the cash flow from operations. Both of these numbers are present on a company's cash flow statement. If there's a wide divergence between this and the payout ratio, you'll need to investigate why this is.

Divergence isn't always a bad thing. It depends on what causes the divergence. If the company has understated its net income, creating a high payout ratio, but still maintains stable cash flow, this is a good situation. However, if cash flow is far less than net income, this is a bad situation. Typically, companies that incur high capital expenditures (such as airlines, oil refining and telecoms) will have much lower free cash flow than net income. This is because capital expenses are not included in the calculation of net income.

Our point here is to tell you that payout ratios and yields are not a quick-fix way of figuring out a business or its dividend quality. A high yield or a low yield isn't "good" or "bad" by itself. You must consider the broader scope of the company and the industry it's in.

Dividend Dates

Dates are all-important when it comes to dividends. The most important date to keep in mind is the ex-dividend date. This is the date you need to be a shareholder in the company to earn a dividend check. Then we have the payment date, which refers to when the dividend will be deposited in your brokerage account and is typically two to three weeks after the ex-dividend date. The date when a company announces a dividend payment is called the announcement date.

For example, at the time of writing, Starbucks' latest ex-dividend date was August 6th, 2020. If you held shares before this date and continued to hold through August 6th, you would receive the dividend. The quarterly dividend was paid on August 21st at a rate of $0.41 per share ($1.64 per share annually, a yield of approximately 1.74%), so if you held 100 shares, you would have received $41. The next ex-dividend date is November 12th, 2020, and the payout date is December 4.

Many short-term traders try to time their stock purchases to collect a dividend payment. We recommend against investing in this manner. It's a good theory on paper, but it almost always fails in real life.

Here's the theory. If you can buy a stock before it goes ex-dividend, and sell it after this date, you can theoretically earn capital gains on the stock's appreciation as well as the dividend. Let's say the dividend yield on the stock is currently five percent. By buying the stock and capturing the dividend, you're capturing at least a five percent gain. This is a huge windfall if you're a short-term trader. A gain of five percent over a few days is well over 200% per year.

However, things are not so simple. Before the ex-dividend date, the price of the stock usually rises to account for the dividend payment. In this case, it will increase by five percent before going ex-dividend. This means short-term traders will buy it for an inflated value.

Once the ex-dividend date passes, the stock declines in value by the same amount. Anyone who bought the stock will therefore suffer a capital loss by selling it at this point. The dividend payment compensates them for it and thus nullifies any gain you can make. It's not impossible to earn a profit doing this. However, you'll also incur higher trading commissions and taxes.

Due to all of these disadvantages, we highly discourage you from adopting such trading tactics. Stick to long-term investing, and you'll make more than enough money to retire comfortably.

DIVIDEND REINVESTMENT

Dividends are powerful for another reason. They allow you to reinvest them and to capture the power of compounding. Every stock or asset that pays a dividend will enable you to reinvest the proceeds through a Dividend Reinvestment Program or DRIP. DRIPs are instituted by the companies you invest in, and are managed through your broker.

Briefly, here's how they work. Let's say you receive a dividend payment of $5 from your investment. If you elect to participate in a DRIP with your broker, they will automatically buy $5 worth of stock in the company for you at no charge. Even brokers who charge you commissions will typically offer this for free because the company is the one that automatically issues equivalent shares of itself to you. All the broker does is record the transaction in your portfolio. You should check with your broker whether they'll charge you fees for this. For example, both Vanguard and TDAmeritrade have free DRIP programs.

Your new shares will be purchased at whatever the stock price is on the payment date. DRIPs are a great way to automate your investing over the long term. You can take advantage of compounding in an entirely passive manner.

There are other advantages of DRIPs as well. Let's say you have $5 but wish to buy shares of a company that's selling for $100 per share. You cannot buy any shares of the company on many broker platforms because you don't have enough money.

Mutual funds allow you to purchase fractional units, but this often isn't possible with common stocks. However, you can buy fractional shares through a DRIP. Some companies even offer special benefits when purchasing through DRIPs. For example, Enterprise Products Partners (EPD), one of our favorite dividend stocks, offers up to a five percent discount on its units for DRIP participants. You can think of this as a five percent built-in gain the moment you buy your new shares.

The younger you are, the more DRIPs make sense. The closer you are to requiring income from your investments, the more it makes sense to withdraw your dividend payouts instead of reinvesting them. You should also check which stocks your broker allows you to DRIP into.

For example, most UK brokers don't allow you to reinvest dividends into US companies automatically. There are also currency restrictions to take into account. European brokers typically allow you to DRIP into stocks denominated in local currencies but not in foreign ones.

Despite these restrictions, DRIPs allow you to automate compounding into your portfolio, and they make a massive difference over the long run. We can illustrate how powerful they are using a simple example.

Let's assume you invest $100,000 by buying an ETF that tracks the S&P 500 and remain invested for 20 years, electing to DRIP your dividends back into the ETF.

We'll use the current average figures and use a steady two percent yield, with the ETF appreciating at an average rate of eight percent per year. How will this investment compare to another where you choose not to reinvest your dividends?

Year	With DRIP	Without DRIP
1	$110,160.00	$108,000.00
2	$121,352.26	$116,640.00
3	$133,681.65	$125,971.20
4	$147,263.70	$136,048.90
5	$162,225.69	$146,932.81
6	$178,707.82	$158,687.43
7	$196,864.54	$171,382.43
8	$216,865.97	$185,093.02
9	$238,899.56	$199,900.46
10	$263,171.75	$215,892.50
11	$289,910.00	$233,163.90
12	$319,364.86	$251,817.01
13	$351,812.33	$271,962.37
14	$387,556.46	$293,719.36
15	$426,932.20	$317,216.91
16	$470,308.51	$342,594.26
17	$518,091.85	$370,001.81
18	$570,729.99	$399,601.95
19	$628,716.15	$431,570.11
20	$692,593.71	$466,095.71

Figure 5: The above table visualized

As you can see, there's a vast difference in the final value of the investment. You'll earn 48% more by reinvesting your dividends over 20 years. We must point out that we've made some assumptions when constructing this table, so you probably won't see these exact numbers. Perhaps our biggest assumption is that the ETF will rise by eight percent every year. This won't happen in real life because there will be years when it will fall, and some years will rise by a greater percentage.

However, over the long run, an 8 percent return is a reasonable expectation. If you elect to DRIP throughout this period, you'll end up buying more units of the ETF when the index is low and less when it's high. This way, your gains will be potentially larger once the index moves back upwards. By looking at things this way, you can begin to understand the power of investing an additional two percent for free every year compared to withdrawing it. You'll build a larger nest egg at the end of your investment period by choosing to reinvest dividends.

5

AVOIDING YIELD TRAPS

A s we mentioned earlier, a considerable problem when investing in dividend-paying assets is that people often confuse high yields with good investment opportunities. Stocks and funds that pay high yields but don't offer any prospect of capital gains are referred to as **yield traps**. You need to avoid them at all costs if you want to be successful. Yield traps are abundant in bear markets since it's during these times that stock prices fall dramatically.

The typical manner in which investors unearth these traps is to set a fixed yield percentage on a stock screener and invest in whatever comes up. For example, you could head over to the FinViz.com stock screener and search for companies that currently have dividend yields greater than five percent.

However, many of these companies are horrible choices for a smart income investor. For example, one particular instrument that has routinely been showing up over the past few years is the Credit Suisse X-Links Crude Oil Shares Covered Call ETN. Assuming you can digest its name, you'll then need to figure out what it does. If you can't, allow us to explain.

ETN stands for Exchange Traded Note and is a type of ETF. The specifics of why this fund is structured as an ETN and not an ETF aren't relevant, but the point is that it behaves like an ETF. You'll notice the term crude oil in its name, and this points to what the fund tracks. This ETN tracks crude oil prices through a relevant index. You'll also notice the term covered call in the ETN's name. This points to what its strategy is.

Covered calls are an options trading strategy. An investor can buy underlying shares of a stock and sell call options on the same stock at higher prices to generate income from it. This is a popular income strategy when executed correctly and the subject of one of our other books, *Covered Calls for Beginners*.

However, while covered calls are a profitable investment strategy, they aren't foolproof. This ETN pays dividends on the profits it makes by implementing the covered call strategy on oil indexes. Its dividend yield is a spectacular 18% and is listed as 26% in some outlets. This discrepancy in itself is an indication that not everything is right with this ETN.

It means it isn't traded often enough and that its prices fluctuate wildly. After all, if dividend payouts remain the same, the only other factor that accounts for different yields is the price. If stock prices can produce yields as far away as six percent from one another, this means prices are jumping all over the place. This is a sure sign of massive volatility, and is the enemy of an income investor.

Why are yields this high anyway? Well, this is because share prices have declined by a whopping 79% over the past year. Not only have prices fallen, but dividend payouts have also reduced as well. The dividend growth over the past three years is -12.27%. This means the most recent payout of $0.45 per share is unlikely to be sustained.

This ETN can be summed up pretty easily. The positives are that it has a great name that you can throw around at cocktail parties and draw impressive nods. The cons are pretty much everything else. It boasts high yields, but the constant capital losses will quickly destroy any yields you'll earn by owning it.

SAFETY AND VALUE TRAPS

A big reason investors go chasing yields over five percent is that they were conditioned to expect such yields from safe investments in the past. For example, savings accounts used to pay four to five percent, with CDs yielding slightly higher amounts. As the yields on these investment options crashed, many investors began searching for the same level of yields without understanding that the safety aspect was gone.

Instead, it's far riskier to invest in instruments that yield such high interest rates. Does this mean it's impossible to find safety in such yields? Hardly. In further chapters, we'll explain how you can screen and install processes to uncover such companies. However, it's equally important for you to understand what an unsafe investment opportunity looks like.

You've just read an example of a dividend trap. A close cousin of the dividend trap is a **value trap**. Value traps are popular in the quantitative value investment community. These investors adhere to the original principles of value investing, as proposed by Benjamin Graham. Graham, who first proposed the system in the late 1930s, sought to identify companies selling for less than the value of their net current assets (NCAV). This value is calculated by subtracting the current liabilities from the current assets.

Graham would then buy companies selling for two-thirds of the price of the NCAV, and buy a lot of them. This gave his portfolio a decent margin of safety. If the company went bust, he wouldn't lose too much money since he bought it at a steep discount. If it did well, he'd net at least a 35% gain since he bought it at 65 cents on the dollar (two-thirds discount.) This investing method is also referred to as "cigar butt investing" and it's a method that Warren Buffett, Graham's most famous student, used to make his first million.

Value Traps

As Buffett discovered, the problem was that such quantitative bargains were harder to come by as time went on. As more people began investing in stocks, good companies were harder to find as the market itself began rising higher. Most of these NCAV stocks were poor companies whose businesses were on a downward spiral. Investors would have to wait until they were liquidated to receive any return on their money.

In many cases, these companies would do nothing. Their share prices would neither rise nor fall, which meant anyone who invested money into these companies would incur massive opportunity costs. Perhaps the most famous cigar butt that Buffett ever invested in was Berkshire Hathaway, which began life as a textile mill on the rocks before transforming into the holding company it is today. That experience, along with Charlie Munger's advice, was more than enough to turn him away from looking for such companies.

Value traps these days are easier than ever to find because they usually pay high dividends. As a result, they yield a high percentage, but the problem is their stock prices either go nowhere or go down. Your money remains stuck in such stocks while the amount of money you'll receive will gradually decrease.

You might be wondering how such companies can pay high dividend amounts? This happens because they typically have a lot of cash on their books. Don't mistake this for a company that generates loads of free cash flow. A value trap company has cash lying dormant on its books. Their primary business is being wound down, and there's nowhere to invest that cash. All the company can do is return it back to investors.

An even worse value trap is the business that is trying to turn itself around but is simply operating in an industry that is going extinct. Japan's stock market famously contained many of these zombie companies in the past 20 years. An investor could have invested in companies with loads of cash on their books thanks to cheap debt, but these companies were operating in head-scratching industries.

Some companies made CDs, and CD players but were pivoting to real estate. There were scaffolding companies who were turning to real estate and making pipes. Electronics companies were pivoting to, you guessed it, real estate. These companies' stock prices rose thanks to prevailing bullish conditions in Japan's stock market, but none of them were making money. You could have earned dividends and capital gains for a few years before everything came crashing down.

This is the most significant risk with value traps. By investing in them, you'll likely earn decent returns initially due to high yields, but the minute the tide turns, you'll see the share price come crashing down, and your gains will be erased. The high dividend yields you earned will not be enough to overcome your capital losses. We'll explain shortly why capital losses (or gains) are more important for you to focus on instead of yields.

Given prevailing market conditions, there will be many of these zombie companies available for you to purchase. They'll have loads of cash on their books, fueled by cheap debt. They will have businesses disrupted thanks to automation, AI or the pandemic and will start paying cash back to investors. They'll cut their dividends at some point, which will send their stock prices crashing, leaving investors with capital losses and extremely low dividend payments. Their yields will remain high though!

Kinder-Morgan

A good example of a company that previously burned its investors is Kinder-Morgan. This wasn't a value trap in the classic sense, but it had all the characteristics of one. Let's begin by looking at what this stock has done since 2014.

Figure 6 - *Weekly Chart of KMI from 2014-2020 (Source: TradingView)*

In Figure 6, note the precipitous drop in share price in early 2015. This is because the board of Kinder-Morgan announced a dividend cut at that time. The dividend yield prior to this cut was eight percent. After the announcement, the effective yield was just two percent. The drop highlights an important point about value and dividend traps.

The stock prices of such companies are routinely inflated, well beyond what their businesses are worth. In the case of Kinder Morgan, every investor was in it for the high yield. Notice that the stock has traded sideways since 2016. COVID-19-induced panic selling did not affect the stock. It merely bounced to a previous low and has half-heartedly stayed there ever since.

Kinder Morgan isn't the only company that has behaved in this manner. Figure 7 illustrates another case.

Figure 7 – Devon Energy Weekly Chart from 2013-2020 (Source: TradingView)

Figure 7 illustrates the behavior of Devon Energy (DVN). Up until 2016, it paid a handsome 26 cents per share dividend. However, you can see that the stock price was falling well before that. This drove yields up massively. Notice the bounce the company experienced in 2016. This was purely because its yield was massive. It was so massive that even a dividend cut to eight cents per share kept its yields high. Prior to 2016, its yield was around two percent.

The stock price rose because of the yield and not due to anything special in Devon's business. Since then, Devon has meandered sideways before moving downwards. Utility stocks such as Devon attract a lot of attention from income investors because they're viewed as a safe haven. This is because utilities are highly regulated, and have high barriers to entry. This leads to steady dividend payments. However, it isn't as simple as that, as the case of Devon Energy illustrates. The stock is down more than 67% from its peak, a loss that will wipe out any gains from dividends.

To drive the point home, let's look at another example and a famous one. Warren Buffett made a huge splash when he bought Heinz in 2015 and then invested more money to merge Kraft Foods with Heinz to create The Kraft Heinz Company. Two venerable food brands combining to create one of the largest conglomerates in history. What could go wrong? Apparently, a lot. Buffett still owns a stake as of this writing but has publicly admitted to over-paying for the company.

Figure 8 illustrates what he has had to go through since investing in the company.

Figure 8: KHC Weekly Chart from 2015-2020 (Source: TradingView)

Notice the peak in 2017? It so happens that towards the end of 2017, the directors of KHC announced they'd have to slash dividends by almost 50% the following year. This led to the stock gradually falling. The company has repeatedly restated its financial results, which indicates a lack of internal audit quality control. For a company of this size, earnings restatements are a huge issue, and the stock's performance has reflected this.

KHC currently pays around $1.10 per year in dividends and yields over five percent. This makes it a high yield stock. However, given its problems and its unwieldy size, clearly, this is a value trap.

Cash Flow and Debt

When looking at these high yield companies, it's best to pay attention to their free cash flows and debt levels. We've already discussed the logic behind looking at free cash flows. After all, without cash, a company can't pay dividends. Why should you pay attention to debt levels, though?

Many companies borrow money from their creditors to finance dividend payments. This is done to maintain a high dividend yield and keep the stock price at a certain level. Boeing has done this recently, as we mentioned previously. Note that there's a lot more to evaluating a company's business than merely looking at increasing debt and dividend payments. In Boeing's case, if the company manages to bounce back and pay dividends from profits, the decision to borrow money to pay dividends would have been a good one. It would have prevented the stock from experiencing volatility.

However, if the company cannot turn itself around, the decision will be painted as a bad one. A lot depends on how the company can execute its strategy. This is why it's critical to look at the business itself instead of merely looking at the numbers.

So now we've ascertained what metrics *don't* matter for dividend growth stocks, let's examine the two which do have an effect.

6

THE 2 METRICS THAT MATTER FOR INCOME INVESTING — PAYOUT RATIOS AND DIVIDEND GROWTH

I f focusing on yields leads you right into a trap, what should you be looking at instead? We've mentioned that you should pay attention to the underlying business, but this is a nebulous criterion. In this chapter, we aim to provide more color on this statement. Specifically, we recommend looking at the dividend payout ratio and the history of dividend growth (or shrinkage.)

Why are these metrics so powerful? For one thing, it's hard to analyze a business with a high degree of accuracy. If you're anything like the average investor, you probably don't have tens of hours to sift through 100+ page annual reports. Dissecting a business fully requires a lot of time and expertise.

In place of that, we need to find suitable metrics that will help us get an accurate picture of a business. They might not provide as deep insight as a full business analysis will, but they will give you 80% of the story in 20% of the time. To expand on this, it's best to turn to what Benjamin Graham once said about figuring out a company's true worth.

These days, the universally accepted method of figuring out a company's true worth is to discount its future cash flows back to the present at an appropriate risk-free hurdle rate. Back in Graham's day though (in the decade after the Great

Depression) this method wasn't widely practiced. Instead, Graham proposed that investors would be better off trying to figure out what something was roughly worth, instead of trying to land on an exact price (Graham & Dodd, 2009).

For example, you might not know what a melon is worth, down to the final cent. If you have the time, you can read weather reports and crop yield surveys and speak to farmers and analyze the quality of the soil. You'll be able to figure out a reasonable price with all this insider knowledge. Or, you can head down to the market and look at the prices. If someone offers you a melon for $100 per lb, you know this is way too much. On the flip side, if you're offered melons at one cent per pound, this seems too little.

Every one of us has a rough idea of what a melon is supposed to cost, given its size. We might not have a precise figure in mind, but we can get in the ballpark. Graham stated that as long as you're in the ballpark and apply an appropriate margin of safety to your purchases, you'll come out ahead in the long run. In his own investing, he had no idea whether the NCAV values he was looking at were legitimate or not. This is why he bought stocks for at least 35% off. That was his margin of safety.

When it comes to dividend stocks, the payout ratio and dividend growth profile get you into the ballpark and provide a decent margin of safety to your investment. You won't know the precise value of your investment by examining these metrics, but as Graham illustrated, you don't need to. This method isn't foolproof, but then again, nothing is. As long as the probability of accuracy is high, it's an excellent method to follow. By repeatedly investing in high probability situations, your likelihood of success will be high. That's how successful investors make money.

PAYOUT RATIOS

The payout ratio is the percentage of net income that is paid as dividends. For example, if a company earns $1.00 per share and pays $0.30 as dividends, its payout ratio is 30%. If it pays $2.00 per share, its payout ratio is 200%.

Payout ratios by themselves are tricky to evaluate. This is because you want to balance a good payout ratio and one that is sustainable. The definition of "good" varies from one company to another. What's good for one company or business might be bad for another. There's also the stage of the company to take into account.

A company that is growing quickly might not be able to sustain a 10% payout. This is because it needs cash to grow. A mature company might not be able to sustain a 90% payout. They might not need all the cash, but this hardly means they don't need any of it. As an income investor, high payout ratios are good for you since it means more income. However, you don't want it to be so high that it begins affecting the company's long-term health.

Ideal Ratios

So what is an ideal ratio? For mature companies, we recommend investing in companies that pay out between 15% and 65% of their net income. Mature companies are the ones that are behemoths in their industries, and that dominate their space. For example, Coca-Cola, Procter & Gamble, and Johnson & Johnson are mature companies. Typically, they have market caps over $100 billion, which makes them mega-cap stocks. The average payout ratio for a Dividend King stock (a company with a record of raising annual dividend payout amounts for at least 50 consecutive years) is 54%.

You can invest in companies that pay more than this, up to a ratio of 75%. For example, Coca-Cola pays out 73% of its net income to investors.

The problem with stable high payout ratio companies is that the market recognizes the value of these stocks and bids prices up. This means the dividend yield on these companies sinks. Coca-Cola is currently yielding 3.25%, which is a good yield, but this is because the pandemic has hit the stock. PepsiCo yields 2.9% but has also been hit by the pandemic, which has artificially inflated yields. Both of these companies usually yield around 1%.

This is why we recommend sticking to companies that pay less than 35% and avoid those that payout more than 55%. If they're bad companies, you'll lose money. If they're stable companies, you can earn higher yields elsewhere, with equally durable companies. The only exception to this rule is REITs, which are mandated to pay out 90% of their net income, so their yields will naturally be higher.

The pandemic has shifted the dividend yield and payout picture considerably. In the REIT sector, yields have gone through the roof, while payouts have also inflated due to lockdowns. Make sure that they're blips caused by the pandemic and aren't indicators of longer-term trends.

In the case of most mature companies, a high payout ratio often indicates a dividend cut is coming. A good example is the professional wrestling company WWE. In June 2011, the company paid 182% of its earnings as dividends while paying out $0.36 per share. The next quarter, they cut the dividend to just $0.12 per share in order to preserve cash. WWE's dividend has remained at that level for the past nine years.

The problem with high (greater than 75%) payout ratios is that they're unsustainable in downturns. Cash is the lifeblood of any business, and by letting it go, companies find themselves precariously perched when things go south. If the payout is unsustainable, the stock nosedives, and investors are left with large unrealized losses on their portfolio.

DIVIDEND GROWTH

The second metric that we can use to evaluate a company's dividend stability is the rate at which payouts have been growing. It's true that when it comes to investing, we're more concerned with the future than the past. However, the past, in this case, can help us approximate the future. A company that has been paying dividends consistently and has also been increasing payouts is undoubtedly a healthy business to invest in.

There's also the fact that such businesses are a rarity, not just in America but in the entire world. By concentrating your money into these companies you can rest assured that you'll be investing in companies with stable businesses that have stood the test of time. This doesn't mean these companies will have posted profits during every single year of their existence. There will be periods where their payout ratios might have moved to unsustainable levels. However, the key is to look at how they rebounded from these tough times. Take the case of AT&T (T) as illustrated in Figure 9.

Figure 9: AT&T's Stock Price & Dividend Payout History from 1991-2021 (source: Macrotrends)

Clearly, there's a trend of increasing dividend payments, which is a good thing. The company is also an undoubtedly mature one in its space. However, its stock price has moved relatively sideways since 1996. This is because the company has regularly paid out a very high proportion of its earnings to shareholders. T's average payout ratio has always hovered over 55%. The board has justified paying such a huge amount because of the cash flow it generates.

Currently, AT&T yields 7.46% (annual dividend payout divided by the current stock price) which is almost equal to the average capital gains that the S&P 500 posts every year. The strong history of dividend payment increases means that the company can support a high payout ratio. Besides, research and development expenses aren't as critical in the telecoms sector. It's not as if AT&T has to develop 5G chips or completely revamp its mobile signal towers and cables to support new tech.

The downside is that you can't expect substantial capital gains in the stock. This is true of pretty much every high yielding dividend stock. However, our aim isn't to capture market leading capital gains. Instead, it's to search for a combination of capital gains and yields that will give us an above-average performance. For example, given AT&T's current yield, all we need is a percentage point increase in the stock price to provide us with a good gain for the year.

Some companies fall into various categories depending on how long they have increased their dividend payouts. Companies that have increased dividends consistently for over 50 years are known as **Dividend Kings**. Procter & Gamble, Coca-Cola, 3M Company, American States Water, and Cincinnati Financial are examples of Dividend Kings.

Those companies that have increased payouts for at least 25 years consecutively are termed **Dividend Aristocrats**. Realty Income, Kimberly-Clark, Clorox, McDonald's, and Genuine Parts Company are examples of such businesses.

Finally, those that have increased their payouts for at least ten years are termed **Dividend Achievers**. Microsoft, Visa, Nike, Best Buy, and Verizon are examples of such companies.

Keep in mind that yield is not a factor in preparing these lists. For example, American States Water yields just 1.74%. The average yield of these companies tends to be low since most people in the market recognize their value. The Achievers tend to yield higher, but this doesn't mean their absolute yield is high. For comparison purposes, the Vanguard Dividend Appreciation ETF (VIG), which tracks the Achievers, yields between 1.5 and 2 percent annually.

This is equal to the average stock yield. ETFs that track the Kings and Aristocrats post similar yields. Typically, capital gains tend to make up for the lack of a yield in such investments. Our point is that despite being stellar dividend providers, Dividend Kings, Aristocrats and Achievers aren't necessarily the best stocks for an income investor.

Instead, you need to focus on the combination of the payout ratio and the history of dividend appreciation. Evaluate both of these factors before deciding to invest. High yields aren't important, but you don't want to be stuck with low yields either. Having said that, investing in a company that has steadily increased dividends is a good way of ensuring your money will remain safe and that you'll earn steady returns.

THE DANGER OF MONTHLY PAYMENTS

There has been an increasing trend in the markets recently of so-called "paycheck stocks." These companies pay their investors monthly dividends instead of quarterly or yearly. Many inexperienced income investors have rushed into these stocks, and their prices have risen as a result. Our advice is to stay away from these kinds of companies. This is because most of them are gimmicks.

A monthly dividend payment is a gimmick by itself. A company that conducts business in hundreds of millions or billions cannot afford to pay cash out every month. It would be impossible for its managers to predict what cash flow would look like over such a short time period. It's a bit like someone asking you how much you can pay them every hour of the day. You wouldn't mind paying a cent every hour, but over time it's going to be tough for you to continually devote resources to paying someone a penny all the time.

In the case of public companies, this burden is even larger. Companies need to announce dividend dates and rework their budgets as of the ex-dividend date. All of this takes time and costs them money. It's a lot easier to pay shareholders once every quarter or yearly, and concentrate on running the business instead.

The only companies who wouldn't mind putting up with all the fuss are those who are looking to inflate their stock prices for some reason. You can bet that these companies have insiders who are looking to get rid of their stock and are using the monthly dividend gimmick to get rid of their holdings for high prices.

Understand that a six percent yield remains the same whether the amount is paid monthly, quarterly, or yearly. You'll still receive six percent of what you invested when you bought the stock. Sure, it's great to receive a check every month, but this should never be your sole reason to invest in a company. The fundamentals matter the most, and you should be taking a look at them before making any investment decision.

We don't mean to say that every company that pays monthly dividends is a bad one. There are certainly a few good ones (one in particular, which we'll be discussing later on). It's just that the very nature of this gimmick attracts certain types of companies. The odds of finding a bad company is higher than finding a good one.

To illustrate this, we'll look at the returns of the Global X SuperDividend ETF (SDIV), the largest of the "Monthly payout" ETFs. In the company's own words, "The Global X SuperDividend® ETF (SDIV) invests in 100 of the highest dividend-yielding equity securities in the world."

The fund attracts many new income investors because of its 8% yield and monthly payouts. However, performance leaves a lot to be desired. The fund is down 34% in the past five years, before management fees. Meaning any potential income gains would have been negated by huge capital losses.

7

HOW CAPITAL GAINS AND DIVIDENDS WORK IN UNISON

Many income investors don't fully grasp how important capital gains are for their portfolios. In their pursuit of income, they routinely capture less than ideal capital gains and end up leaving a lot of money on the table. Even worse, they might find themselves in dividend or value traps where they earn a steady income, which is then negated by huge capital losses.

It's important to understand that capital gains are just as important as any interest or dividend income you earn from your investments. An excellent example of the role of capital gains is to look at the world of junk bond investing.

Junk bonds are termed as such because they pay a high coupon (interest rate). Every bond is provided a rating by the investment rating agencies, and bonds with a rating below B are considered junk. Junk bonds are mostly issued by bad companies, but good companies issue them as well. Usually, good companies' junk bonds are either redeemed early or are converted to common stock before maturity.

Why are these bonds rated as junk in the first place? Simply put, companies either don't have the cash to pay interest until maturity, or these bonds are known as "junior debt", which means the company doesn't prioritize repaying them. Junior debt often gets converted to equity, which means you are better off buying the stock of the company instead of the junk debt.

To compensate investors for these risks, companies attach high coupon rates to junk debt. It's not uncommon to see coupons of 12-15% attached to junk bonds. This sounds like a great deal to uninformed investors.

You hear the word bond and think safety and see 15% coupons and see dollar signs. So you buy junk debt, and before you know it, the company defaults on payments, leaving you with nothing.

You see, with junk bonds, there is almost no hope of earning capital gains, but there is close to a 100% chance of earning a capital loss. Bond prices are quoted as percentages, so let's look at an example.

If a bond's price is $1,000 and the coupon rate is 15%. Your annual interest payment will be $150.

If that same bond is trading at 65 (65% of its value,) you're getting a lower price on an asset and thus your relative interest rate will be higher. So your $1,000 bond now costs $650 and your $150 annual payout is now at a rate of 23% ($150/$650).

However, once the company defaults, your bond is going to be worth zero. This means you'll earn a capital loss of 55%. How does an income gain of 23% compare against that? It hardly compensates you for the risk of losing 55%. You'll need to buy the bond for less than the coupon percentage to compensate you for the risk, and no company or investor is going to sell junk that low unless default is imminent.

As you can see, capital losses always overshadow income gains. There is also another reason we're highlighting junk bonds. In low interest rate environments like we are in now, junk bonds become more popular. Cash-strapped companies know that investors are hungry for income, and they begin issuing junk debt to capture whatever money they can quickly. The stock market equivalent for such behavior is to split stock when euphoria and blind optimism are at an all-time high. It costs companies nothing, and the euphoria or desire to earn more money drives interest.

Watch out for advertisements pushing junk bonds towards you over the next few years. They'll often be advertised as "high income" or "high yield" instruments but will more than generate less money for you in the long term when compared with a stock that offers a balance of capital gains and dividends.

CAPITAL GAINS IN STOCKS

While junk bonds have almost no hope of earning a capital gain, stocks can potentially earn them at all times.

In fact, when it comes to stocks, capital gains are the primary drivers of wealth. The stock market rises at an average of 8 to 10 percent every year, while the average dividend yield is around two percent. Clearly, a gain or loss of eight percent every year overrides income gains of two percent. Let's look at an example to see how this works. The table below illustrates the difference between a stock that gains 10% per year on average but pays just one percent in dividends, versus another stock that yields eight percent but gains only one percent every year. Our initial investment is $100,000.

Year	10% Gains/ 1% Yield	1% Gains/ 8% Yield
1	$111,000.00	$109,000.00
2	$123,210.00	$118,810.00
3	$136,763.10	$129,502.90
4	$151,807.04	$141,158.16
5	$168,505.82	$153,862.40
6	$187,041.46	$167,710.01
7	$207,616.02	$182,803.91
8	$230,453.78	$199,256.26
9	$255,803.69	$217,189.33
10	$283,942.10	$236,736.37
11	$315,175.73	$258,042.64
12	$349,845.06	$281,266.48
13	$388,328.02	$306,580.46
14	$431,044.10	$334,172.70
15	$478,458.95	$364,248.25
16	$531,089.43	$397,030.59
17	$589,509.27	$432,763.34
18	$654,355.29	$471,712.04
19	$726,334.37	$514,166.13
20	$806,231.15	$560,441.08

It's clear that there's a big difference between the two columns. Despite investing in a high yield stock, your portfolio grows to just $560,441 compared to $806,231. The question of where to invest your money isn't as straightforward, though. A lot depends on your priorities too. While the first choice makes you more money, you'll earn just one percent as cash flow.

This isn't enough for income investors under any circumstances. You'll earn a large check every year with the second choice, but your investment isn't growing as quickly. The ideal investment would combine the first option's capital gains and the yield of the second, but such investments are exceedingly rare.

The point of this example is to illustrate that capital gains are just as powerful as dividend yields. And yet, there's another issue with high yields. The real amount you'll earn from the second investment will be lower than what's indicated due to ordinary income taxes you'll pay on your investment. Your eight percent yield will be reduced to 6.4% after taxes. Capital gains aren't taxed until you sell your investment. This means you can compound your money freely. You can't compound your money to the same extent with dividends because you'll pay taxes every year. This happens even if you DRIP your payments back into the stock, which we've assumed in this example.

8

THE 11 PRINCIPLES FOR FINDING GREAT DIVIDEND PAYING STOCKS

Now that you've learned what NOT to look at when searching for dividend-paying stocks, it's time to develop a process that will help you find the best dividend paying stocks in the market.

In our previous book *The 8 Step Beginner's Guide to Value Investing* we defined a rational process that helps you discover great stocks for the long term. We're going to stick to the same base formula when it comes to dividend investing.

This is because evaluating a good dividend-paying stock isn't that much different from evaluating a stock for long-term investing. In the latter case you'll be content with earning capital gains while in the former case you'll need the stock to pay you dividends. This means the bulk of our process is pretty much the same, except we need to add one additional criterion to find good dividend-paying stocks.

Let's go through all of these criteria one by one.

PRINCIPLE ONE: THE WARREN BUFFETT TEST

This principle runs extremely deep. There are many consequences of following this rule, and by itself it'll help you avoid many of the pitfalls that individual investors face. The rule itself is simple. Always treat your investments as if you're buying a business. You're not buying stock or buying shares but are grabbing a piece of a living, breathing business that has employees, profits, and office space. This means you need to act like a business owner and not as a speculator.

Speculation in this context refers to implementing money-making schemes that contain high risk with an uncertain reward. For example, buying a stock because it's about to go ex-dividend is a speculative practice. The same applies if you buy the stock just before an important interest rate announcement because you expect a rate hike to benefit its prospects over the next year.

As a rule of thumb, if your investment horizon is less than ten years long, you are more likely speculating rather than investing. We're not saying you need to hold onto your investment for that entire period. Instead we're saying you need to evaluate what the business will look like over the next decade at the very least. Since you can't predict macroeconomic factors very well over the next decade, the only solution is to turn to business fundamentals.

This is how smart business owners think of their enterprises. You are unlikely to find the owner of a company selling their stake in their company because they are facing a few macroeconomic headwinds. Neither do they plan to repurchase it on the cheap once it falls from a high sale price. This kind of owner won't have time to run everyday operations, producing earnings and revenues

Yet, many investors behave in this manner. At the mere hint of economic uncertainty, they run for the hills and the stock price crashes. Ask yourself this: If you bought a company for $100 per share and if the business fundamentals remain the same while the stock price crashes to $50, would you buy or sell? A business owner would always buy in this situation. If the business was a good buy at $100, it's an even better buy at $50. The company's fundamentals are the same, so what does it matter what the stock price is?

Buffett's mentor Benjamin Graham has an interesting way of describing the above situation. He envisioned a situation where the investor owned an important asset that they had bought for a price, say $100. Every day a person named Mr. Market would walk up to them and offer the investor a price for that asset. Mr. Market was a bit of a manic depressive and would one day offer $40 for the asset, and the next day would offer $1,000. There was never any rhyme or reason behind his prices.

This is how the stock market behaves. Buffett has also spoken of how people view real estate property prices compared to how we view stock prices. If you owned a piece of land, would you consider buying it today and selling it tomorrow, only to repurchase it on the third day? It's absurd! Neither would you check what the property is worth every single day.

Yet so many investors do this with stocks because they view them as mere numbers on a screen. By engaging in such short-term behavior, you increase your likelihood of making poor decisions. Market timing is also not as easy as it sounds on paper. No one, not even the best paid Wall Street pros who spend their entire lives painstakingly analyzing chart patterns and order flows, can time the top of a market or its bottom. If someone could do this with perfect accuracy just 2-3 times in a row, they'd likely be the richest person alive.

In reality, the richest person alive, Jeff Bezos, is a business owner who has held his favorite stock (Amazon) for more than 20 years. This is why it's best to stick to a company's fundamentals and treat it as an asset, not as a piece of paper.

PRINCIPLE TWO: UNDERSTAND THE BUSINESS THOROUGHLY

Businesses are complicated creatures. They aren't always what they seem on the surface. For example, McDonald's is seemingly a fast food company, but its real business lies in real estate. Similarly, Starbucks is a coffee chain, but its real business is a cheap source of entertainment and socializing, along with serving as a makeshift office and meeting room for people.

As a business owner, you need to drill deep into how a company makes money. The business environment that companies face is challenging, and over time almost all of them have to adapt, or they die out. Even a company that is in a seemingly simple business such as Coca-Cola has to adapt. In Coca-Cola's case, it's easy to think they could simply keep producing Coke and leave it at that. However, with people becoming increasingly conscious of the environmental impact of their choices and becoming more health-conscious, how much longer can Coca-Cola rely on sugary syrup?

This is why Coca-Cola owns more than 500 brands worldwide. It's also why PepsiCo long ago diversified its business by purchasing FritoLay, which is the world's largest producer of snacks. If a soft drink manufacturer faces such challenges, imagine the challenges that a more sophisticated business faces. As an investor, you don't need to figure out how companies should react to such environments, but you do need to know where the business makes its money.

For example, a PepsiCo shareholder who doesn't understand that their dividends come largely from the snack business doesn't understand how their company works. Why is it so vital for you to understand the business? After all, isn't that management's job? It's important for you as an investor to understand it too because this prevents you from selling or buying at inopportune moments.

For example, Coca-Cola's stock sank after the market crash of 1987. Millions of Coca-Cola shareholders sold their shares. Warren Buffett instead went out and bought as much of the company as he could lay his hands on. Today he owns close to 10% of the company, having paid $1.8 billion for his stake, as a result. Berkshire Hathaway earns $640 million in Coca-Cola dividends alone every year (*Here's How Much Warren Buffett Has Made on Coca-Cola*, 2019).

Berkshire has earned over seven billion dollars in dividends from its investment in Coca-Cola. That's just dividends. It doesn't include capital gains from the 1,750% rise in Coca-Cola's stock since 1989. What's the key behind such monstrous gains? Buffett understood how Coca-Cola makes money and the advantageous way it had structured its relationships with its bottlers.

To understand a business, you need to understand the sector it operates in and how the economics of that sector work. Some sectors are allergic to money. For example, with the exception of companies like Southwest Airlines, the commercial airline business has long been a terrible place to invest money.

However, commercial airplane manufacturers have always had profitable businesses, their current troubles notwithstanding. Similarly, cruise ship operators have always had to deal with tough business conditions. Cruise ship builders? Not so much.

A similar example is in the mobile phone industry. The tussle between Apple and Samsung has always grabbed headlines. However, the glass on both phones comes from the same company: Corning Inc (GLW), whose stock has doubled over the past five years while still paying around a 2.5-3% dividend.

Intelligent investors understand that great companies are still subject to their industries' economics. Sometimes it's better to invest in shovels than dig for gold yourself.

PRINCIPLE THREE: UNDERSTAND THE RELATIONSHIP BETWEEN THE BUSINESS & THE SECTOR

A rising tide lifts all boats. Bull markets have always operated on these terms and have made even the most unintelligent speculators lots of money. However, once the tide goes out, we get to see who's well-positioned and who isn't. Sector growth often lifts every single company operating within it, irrespective of whether these companies make money or not.

In our previous book, we highlighted the case of 5G stocks, but since then, we've been presented with an even better example: the electric vehicle market. Nothing makes sense when it comes to EVs anymore. It began with Tesla, a company that for years existed solely on the promise of "what if", since it took 16 years to make a profit. The company was formed in 2003, and it posted its first profit in 2019. It's since posted consecutive quarterly profits, which is a great thing for investors, and will likely end 2020 with its first-ever annual profit.

The company's lifeblood is the subsidies it receives from the government for selling energy credits to other manufacturers. Without this subsidy, the company continues to lose money with every car it produces. However, at least Tesla has a good product, real customers, the best technology in the sector, and a visionary leader.

The same can't be said of other EV manufacturers. The events that recently engulfed alleged electric truck maker Nikola (NKLA) were a good example. The company made the headlines in the middle of 2020 after its stock price soared 3,000% in a matter of days. However, this was illustrative of how irrational markets can be in the short term, and the company's fortunes began unraveling from there.

On September 10th, 2020, a report compiled by Hindenburg Research showed that Nikola's products were nonexistent and that their Nikola One semi-truck was functional only if it was plugged into a wall outlet, amongst other lies. This resulted in GM pulling out of a deal to buy the company, and led to CEO and Founder Trevor Milton being forced to resign.

Other EV startups that have reached multi-billion-dollar valuations are Hyllion, Fisker, Karma, Workhorse, and Spartan. Fisker interestingly has been around since 2007, went bust in between, and has since made a comeback. Sounds like a great story, except, the comeback was primarily because of the huge surge of interest in EVs, prompting the founders to cash in on the boom and raise money. The company produced a car back in the day that rivalled Tesla's Roadster but was even more unreliable than its competitor.

These examples demonstrate that the EV sector is a perfect example of how unprofitable and fundamentally flawed companies benefit from generally favorable business conditions. You need to look underneath the hood to reveal which companies have staying power and which are built on thin air.

PRINCIPLE FOUR: IT'S A NEWER COMPANY, THE FOUNDER SHOULD STILL BE INVOLVED

The time it takes these days for a company to go public has decreased significantly. Even as recently as the 1990s, companies had to prove a significant level of profits and revenues before considering listing themselves on exchanges. Over and above listing requirements, the Initial Public Offering (IPO) process was tough and required a ton of regulatory documentation. IPOs also cost a lot, and most companies couldn't afford them.

These days, thanks to reverse merger processes and Special Purpose Acquisition Companies (SPACs), the time it takes to go public is shorter than what it used to be. We're witnessing more companies go public in the earlier stages of their lives. As a result, the market has become more unstable since you have billion-dollar companies that are essentially startups.

In such environments with younger companies, it's imperative that you evaluate whether the founder is still on board. The founder's presence mitigates much of the risk that these companies pose to investors because the person with the grand vision is still on board. The founder is the one who has been there since the beginning and is the person most responsible for steering the company this far. They're also the true visionaries who can help guide the company through tough times.

Take the case of Apple and Steve Jobs. Around the turn of the millennium, Apple was a distant second to Microsoft, and closing the gap seemed hopeless. Only a founder such as Jobs could have turned the business around by changing the rules completely. He turned Apple from a computer company to a communications product manufacturing company. As a result, after dominating for several years in its field, Microsoft found itself playing the wrong sport entirely.

This pivot wasn't entirely original, unlike popular imagination suggests. Sony had been making phones, computers, and electronics for many years. However, it hadn't experienced anywhere close to Apple's eventual success. The reason was primarily that Apple had the advantage of being guided by its founder through a new market and developing unique philosophies and business processes that allowed it to thrive.

Technology companies face many hurdles, and it's essential that their founders remain close to the company. With many of the trailblazers now growing older, this is more important than ever. The fact that Bill Gates wasn't present to counter Jobs and the ascent of Google and Facebook hampered Microsoft for over a decade. To its credit, the firm has bounced back admirably thanks to its shift in focus to the cloud computing business. However, one wonders how much further ahead they might have been with Gates on board.

PRINCIPLE FIVE: INTANGIBLE ASSET ADVANTAGE

A company's balance sheet lists all of its assets and liabilities. The most interesting section, and the one most ripe for manipulation, is the intangible assets section. This is where the company lists the assets that don't have a specific monetary value attached to them. For example, Coca-Cola's brand name is an intangible asset. If you were to pour Coke into a bottle branded as "Bubba's Cola," it's unlikely to sell in the same volumes.

It isn't just the brand name but the colors, the script, the taste of the product, and 60+ years of feelings brought upon customers by global advertising that is an intangible asset. Coca-Cola also owns the patent on its formula as well as trademarks on its name and brand products. All of these are extremely valuable to the company. Without these intangible assets, Coca-Cola would likely be a pretty ordinary business.

So why are intangible assets so highly valued? Put simply, they signify competitive advantages that cannot be quickly eroded. It's easy to create a better formula than Coca-Cola's. Well, not easy, but it's certainly within the realm of possibility.

However, what constitutes better? More importantly, how does one go about overcoming how consumers feel when they look at the Coca-Cola brand and the red labeling? It's close to impossible to push a new brand as being more attractive.

Many pharmaceutical companies operate in this manner, as well. Despite the field relying heavily on disruptive inventions, few staple companies dominate the industry. Every now and then, one gains the upper hand over another, but in the long run, all of them remain roughly in position. This is because of the large hoard of intellectual property (IP) they own. Intellectual property is an intangible asset and includes patents, formulas, and designs. The patent libraries that these firms hold are enough to drive billion-dollar valuations by themselves.

The computing industry, or at least the companies which dominated the early internet era, are heading to a similar structure. The likes of Google, Apple, Amazon, Facebook, and Microsoft own vast patent libraries, and it's hard to see how these companies will ever be disrupted in the future. This illustrates how strong the effect of intangible assets is.

PRINCIPLE SIX: UPPER MANAGEMENT IS BOUGHT IN

If you ask a CEO of any public company if they are focused on the long term goals of the company, it's likely that at least 95% would say yes. However, in reality, actions speak louder than words. This is why we like to take a more quantitative look at management's goals. We do this by looking at how management is compensated to get a deeper insight into where their incentives lie.

For starters, you should look at companies that have a good amount of insider ownership. Insiders constitute a company's officers, directors and C-Level executives (and their families), who have access to key company information before the general public. If these people, who theoretically should know more about the company than anyone else, have enough confidence in the company to place their own money in the stock, then that's a positive sign.

In public companies, insider ownership (the total percentage of shares held by insiders) greater than 20% is considered extremely high.

To check what percentage of a company is owned by insiders, you can go to Yahoo Finance, select your company of choice and click on the Holding tab.

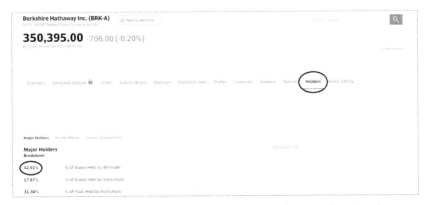

Figure 10: The insider ownership for Berkshire Hathaway (Source: Yahoo Finance)

High insider ownership far greater than 20% isn't always a good thing. When it's that high, it is difficult for shareholders to have any say over management and changes can be hard to implement. If the company with high insider ownership is being run inefficiently, then as a shareholder, you won't be able to do anything.

So always look for a good amount of insider ownership but not too much. Some institutional presence is positive unless the company is too small to be attractive to a large institution. However, too much institutional ownership makes the company subject to activist investors. This is where hedge funds with large ownership stakes will pressure the company's board of directors to make changes to increase short term profits.

Look at management compensation structure as well. Companies explicitly list this out in their annual reports (10-K). A compensation structure that is primarily based on stock options is a good sign since this incentivizes executives to reward investors.

Just as with insider ownership, though, there's a possibility to go overboard with this. If executive compensation is tied directly to stock prices, executives are incentivized to maximize stock prices. The short term performance of a company's stock and its long run profitability are two different things. In the long run, they converge, but in the short term they don't. Management that is primarily focused on quarterly stock performance is not setting the company up for long-term success.

Look for stock options being awarded a few years down the line instead of being awarded over the short term. Another important factor to look for is the impact of issuing options on shareholders' equity. Typically options are expensed, and this amount needs to be a reasonable charge. If it significantly detracts from earnings, then it's probably excessive.

This isn't always possible to figure out, but take a look at the severance packages that are being offered to departing executives. Many CEOs collect tens of millions in compensation even after doing a bad job. You won't be able to get details on individual contracts, but if the company has a history of making poor deals with its executives, this means the Board of Directors isn't doing their jobs properly. Stay away from such companies.

Twenty years ago, to find real time information on insider ownership, you would have needed a Bloomberg terminal, or you would have had to wait weeks for your broker to send you the information in the mail. Fortunately for you, technology is a great equalizer, and now you can instantly access the same information for free.

The two best websites to find data on insider ownership for free are FinViz.com and GuruFocus.com – both of which track trades made by company insiders. If you see the company CEO buying stock, that's an excellent sign. After all, if a CEO is confident enough in the company's long term outlook to put their own money on it, that's a glowing recommendation.

We should note that while insider buying is usually a positive sign, insider selling is less of an indicator of the long-term prospects of a company. Insider sales are often made for reasons beyond the person's expectations for the company. It is often as simple as a board member wanting the cash to purchase a new home.

PRINCIPLE SEVEN: THE COMPANY HAS STRONG ADVERTISING, MARKETING & SALES OPERATIONS

A company might have a great product or service, but all those pretty features are of no use if they cannot sell it, which means that sales and marketing are the lifeblood of every organization.

A sign of a company with strong sales and marketing is increasing revenues. While profits can be massaged, revenues are quite basic and cannot be fudged without doing something grossly illegal. If you see healthy growth in revenues year after year, and if these revenues are keeping up with net income increases, this is a good sign. Another positive indicator is low turnover within the upper management of the sales and marketing departments.

Since net income can be massaged to make it look better than it is, it's a good idea to look at free cash flow and compare that to increases in revenues. If revenue increases aren't resulting in higher free cash flows, either the company is reinvesting vast amounts of cash into capital expenses, or they're employing some creative accounting with regards to recognizing revenues. If you aren't sure where to find these numbers in a company's financial statements, make sure you grab a copy of our free video course *Company Valuation 101*, which shows you exactly where to find these numbers.

You can get the course as part of your bonus resources by going to https://freemanpublications.com/bonus

To figure out marketing strategies, read a company's press releases and new product or service announcements. Sure, there will be a lot of fluff in these releases, but you'll get a good idea of how a company is positioning itself in the market.

PRINCIPLE EIGHT: MANAGEMENT IS WILLING TO MAKE SHORT-TERM SACRIFICES FOR LONG-TERM RESULTS

As a long-term investor, your focus is going to last longer than ten years. It stands to reason that you want management that is equally focused over the long term. Company executives need to balance both the short and long-term demands of their businesses. An excellent example of this is happening with Disney right now.

In July 2020, Disney made a stunning announcement when it decided to forego paying its dividend. This saved the company $1.6 billion in cash. With its businesses being hit hard by the pandemic, any reasonable investor and business owner would have applauded this move. However, the market being what it is, rewarded Disney with a tumble in stock price. Naturally, long-term focused investors could have taken advantage of this opportunity to buy more.

This particular decision was made keeping in mind the medium-term effects on the company's profitability. With the majority of its business coming from parks and entertainment while facing uncertain reopening times, it stands to reason that Disney's executives would choose to hang on to cash to weather tough times.

However, an even bigger decision is looming ahead for Disney. The company has been robust enough to begin diversifying beyond its traditional parks and entertainment model. The launch of Disney+ was such a move. With streaming picking up the pace and with the vast inventory of IP that the company has, releasing entertainment directly onto streaming services makes a lot of sense. As the pandemic has ravaged other areas of Disney's business, Disney+ remains a bright spot and offers enormous potential.

It's so huge that prominent institutional investor and Disney shareholder Dan Loeb wants the company to forego its dividend entirely and devote more cash towards developing Disney+ (de Haas, 2020). If management follows through on this, they'll be explicitly prioritizing the long term and will hurt their short-term prospects.

A good management team will create a balance between the two while leaning towards the long term. Regardless of how the situation at Disney plays out, there is no doubt that the company has management that seeks to create value for the long term above all else. There aren't many managers who will willingly cut their dividend entirely and risk a tumbling stock.

One of the best metrics to look at the long-term orientation of a company's management is to look at the return on equity that the managers have generated. You calculate this by dividing earnings by the shareholders' equity as listed in the balance sheet. Long-term-oriented management continually reinvests profits to create better assets. The better their reinvestment decisions are, the better the assets that they create. This is what drives long-term earnings growth.

Stability in management is also an essential quality to look for. Many companies have long-standing CEOs, but the people around them come and go frequently. High executive turnover is a hallmark of a CEO who pushes blame onto his/her subordinates and doesn't accept it themselves. Instead of looking at how long the CEO has been there, look for low turnover in the company's upper echelons and whether the organization has a succession plan for when the current CEO leaves.

General Electric is a famous example of how future CEOs are groomed in the final years of the previous CEO's tenure. Steve Jobs also spent many of his last years at Apple preparing Tim Cook to step into the CEO role. A position that Cook himself now finds himself in as he enters his 10th year as the company's leader.

Developing a core management team is a sign of preparing for the long term. The founder won't always be around, so there has to be someone to pick up the slack. The stronger the team is, the stronger the organization is.

PRINCIPLE NINE: THE COMPANY HAS AN ECONOMIC MOAT

The concept of the economic moat was popularized by Warren Buffett and his business partner Charlie Munger. They preferred investing in companies that had some sort of unfair (but legal) advantage in the way they ran their business. Coca-Cola has an unfair advantage by being around for so long and having a fully recognizable brand name. See's Candies, a highly publicized Berkshire Hathaway investment, has a strong brand name as well. So does GEICO and other companies that they've invested in over the years.

A moat comes in many forms. Walmart's moat is the high economies of scale it achieves, enabling it to slash prices to levels that are unsustainable for smaller competitors. A local store cannot buy inventory in the volumes that Walmart does and cannot reduce prices to that extent. This naturally eliminates competition. Amazon enjoys similar advantages in the online retail space.

Google and Facebook enjoy another type of moat, which is increasingly relevant in the digital business era. This is referred to as the network effect. The more that people use a company's product, the better the product becomes. For example, compared to these days, Google's search algorithm was extremely rudimentary when it debuted. However, as more people used Google, the more data it could collect, the more its algorithm learned human speech patterns and search tendencies. For companies like Google, more users equal greater profits.

Similarly, Facebook derives most of its market value from its large user base. The more that users stay on the platform, the greater the quantity of data that Facebook collects. This insight allows Facebook to provide better targeting services for advertisers, which fuels ad spend on the platform.

For example, a Facebook advertiser can elect to show their ads only to female small business owners aged between 35-44, who live in Los Angeles. When you compare that level of specificity to TV or print advertising, it's easy to see why total advertising spend on Facebook has increased by 400% over the past five years.

The network effect is tough for competitors to overcome since they cannot merely improve on an existing product. They need to reinvent the entire business model.

Businesses that have economic moats survive tough times better than ones that don't. The opposite of a company that has a moat is one that sells a commodity product. A commodity product is one that differentiates itself solely on its price. For example, if you were in the market for a new mouse for your laptop, you're going to choose one that is ergonomic and effective but only up to a certain price. Another example is the pen you choose to write with.

On the face of it, Walmart has a commodity product. The only reason people shop there is that they offer the cheapest goods. However, there's a difference between selling products that are differentiated solely on price versus what Walmart does. Walmart consistently delivers the cheapest goods, no matter the broader economic conditions. There is no other business in America that can do this as efficiently as Walmart does. Thus, the moat it has doesn't have to do with price. It's more about how Walmart conducts its processes that ensure it can offer the lowest price all the time.

Other examples of moats are companies operating in non-sexy industries. Unattractive industries are great because companies receive less analyst attention, they are less prone to disruption, and the incumbents can often have a natural monopoly.

A great example of this is Waste Management. You don't have to be a genius to figure out which industry the company is in. Now imagine being an employee of Waste Management. If you met someone at a barbecue, would you introduce yourself as your job title "I work in marketing," or would you let them know you work for a company called Waste Management?

In addition, there aren't too many 20somethings in Silicon Valley spending all night hyped up on caffeine and Adderall hypothesizing on how to disrupt the waste management industry. That is a big reason why the stock is up 400% in the past decade while simultaneously increasing its dividend payouts.

Another factor that can cause a moat is a company operating in a morally or ethically dubious industry. Tobacco, alcohol, and casino companies all fall under this category.

We should note that you should never compromise your moral or ethical views just to make money. The beauty of long term investing is that you can eliminate pretty much any industry you *don't* want to invest in but still make a killing in sectors that do fit within your views or beliefs.

PRINCIPLE TEN: THE BUSINESS CAN WEATHER A STORM

Anyone can make money when times are good. However, it's a sign of strength when businesses can thrive during downturns. We don't mean to say that you should look at businesses that benefit from downturns, such as collection agencies or receivables financing companies. These industries benefit when things are bad but are depressed when conditions are good.

Instead, your task is to search for companies that do well when times are good and bad. Walmart is a good example of such a business. When times are good, it does decently since everyone needs cheap groceries and goods. When times are rough, it does even better. Compare them to the likes of The Fresh Market and other high-end grocers, and you'll see the difference. While the quality of food at the latter supermarkets is undoubtedly better, your concern as an investor is the business and its economics.

There are some key factors you can look at when figuring out how recession-proof a business is. Look at the number of suppliers and customers it has. Companies will disclose this in the introduction of their annual 10-K filings. If more than 90% of revenues derive from a single customer, this is a very bad sign. Remember, public companies on average sell hundreds of millions of dollars worth of products and services per year. If a single customer drives 90% of this revenue, what's going to happen if that customer hits a rough patch?

Similarly, having just one supplier is a risky move. In some industries, having a single supplier is a feature, not a bug. However, even in these businesses, managers typically have backup plans to mitigate the loss of a supplier. This is why the troubles that befell Intel over the past few years haven't affected their customers too much. They had backup suppliers ready to go.

Lastly, leverage is an especially relevant feature to consider. Leverage refers to the ratio of debt to equity on a company's balance sheet. In our current low interest rate environments, companies have taken on huge levels of debt since it's cheap. With the Fed indicating that they'll be maintaining low interest rates for the foreseeable future, this might lead to management taking things easy and underestimating the risk of overleveraging themselves.

The best way to think about leverage is to compare it to an investment you might routinely make. Let's take the case of a house you buy. If the home is worth $100,000 and you borrow $90,000 to finance it, you own just 10% of the property. If you rent the property out to pay for the monthly mortgage, this looks like a great decision. However, what happens when your tenant moves out and you can't find someone else? All those mortgage payments will come out of your pocket, and if you can't afford to make them, the house gets foreclosed.

This is pretty much what happens to companies as well. The tricky thing with companies is that they need to service debt from revenues. Due to the very nature of the business, revenues will move up and down. It's not as if companies can accurately predict what might happen tomorrow. Look at the number of bankruptcies and layoffs that occurred due to the pandemic-enforced lockdowns. This is a surefire indicator of how companies have overleveraged themselves to the point that two to three months' worth of lockdowns toppled them into the red.

It's a bit like a household not having enough emergency cash to pay for three months' worth of living expenses, which is extremely risky. As investors, we often pay special attention to the good times but neglect the bad. An intelligent investor always considers risk above reward. Eliminate how you could lose money, and you'll automatically start making money.

PRINCIPLE ELEVEN: IMPLEMENT THE 10-10-10 RULE

The ten preceding criteria were presented in our book *The 8 Step Beginner's Guide to Value Investing*. For Dividend Growth investing, we can now present the 11th factor to help guide your investment process. This is the 10-10-10 rule.

The first factor to look for in a company is **paying dividends for the past ten years**. This is a minimum criterion, so the longer the dividend payment record is, the better.

Next, you want to look for companies that have **consistently grown their dividend payouts over the past ten years**. We're not talking about massive increases in yield but sustainable ones. A stable and slowly increasing payout points to a stable stock price and solid long term company prospects.

Lastly, you should look for companies that can conceivably **grow their stock prices for the next ten years**. It's no use getting healthy dividend payments if your capital is being eroded by a declining stock price. This is why it can be helpful to look for stocks that have had their prices beaten down recently. If it's a high quality company, its prospects of increasing in value over the next decade are much better.

With all of these principles in mind, we're now ready to present the best income investment candidates for your portfolio.

9

THE 7 BEST DIVIDEND GROWTH STOCKS FOR 2021 AND BEYOND

B efore we dive in, we'd like to start by saying certain sectors gravitate more towards a balance of dividends and capital gains. These are energy, financials, and pharmaceuticals. We'll also include REITs in there, but we'll discuss REITs in more detail in the next chapter.

Generally speaking, if a company isn't in one of these sectors, you should avoid dividend yields of greater than four percent. AT&T is the most famous exception to this, but many investors fall into yield traps when seeking income-producing stocks outside of these sectors.

THE BEST HIGH YIELD STOCKS TO INVEST IN

Of the non-penny stocks listed in the United States, 1,982 stocks currently pay a dividend of over one percent.

Change that to five percent, and the number goes down to 526. Of those 526, we want to identify stable companies whose earnings are growing. This is because we want to pick companies that can reliably pay high dividends for the foreseeable future while also offering capital gains potential. From that list of 526, we've selected seven stocks which meet these criteria.

AbbVie Inc. (NYSE:ABBV)

Market Cap - $148 billion

52 week high/low - 101.28/62.55

Current yield - 5.14%

Beta - 0.69

Number of years of dividend increases - 47

While AbbVie has only been operating as an independent company for seven years, it has long been a staple of the pharmaceutical industry. The company was spun off from its parent Abbott Labs in 2013. AbbVie has a long and profitable track record extending back to its days as a division of its larger parent company. Abbott Labs spun its research-based pharmaceutical manufacturing business, and AbbVie was the result.

The company is best known for its Humira medication, which is used to treat rheumatoid arthritis, Crohn's disease, and ulcerative colitis. Humira is the biggest money spinner for the company and accounts for as much as 50% of the company's revenues. Going back to our principles in the previous chapter, this might seem like a huge risk. However, we still like AbbVie because the dependence on Humira is shrinking. In 2018, the percentage of revenues that Humira accounted for was 65%.

The pharma industry can present cyclical advantages for the firms operating in it due to the way patents work. The typical cycle runs something like this. A firm pours resources into developing a drug and, after lengthy trials, is granted permission to mass manufacture it. The patent on the drug lasts for around 20 years, giving the firm a monopoly in the developed world.

As the 20-year cycle ends, the firm usually has other drugs in development, and this starts another 20-year monopoly on the formulation. This doesn't mean the firm has a monopoly on how the disease is treated. Other firms can step in with their own formulations. However, the combination of treatment periods and side effects causes one drug to be favored over another. Sales and marketing also play an important role with sales reps routinely keeping tabs on what doctors are prescribing their patients.

Coming back to AbbVie, the patent on Humira expires in 2023, and this might be a cause for concern for a smaller firm. However, AbbVie has other drugs poised to take over the heavy lifting. The firm produces drugs such as Imbruvica and Venclexta that are used to treat blood cancer and are prescribed routinely. Other immunology drugs such as Rinvoq and Skyrizi are also poised to take over the space.

Moving away from the product specifics, the financials of the company are robust. It has reported positive cash flow for the past ten quarters and has no significant litigation expenses. This is a huge plus. In comparison, Johnson & Johnson spent $5.1 billion in lawsuit-related expenses in 2019. Since splitting from Abbott Labs, AbbVie's stock has grown by 160% and has maintained high dividend payouts.

Thanks to its association with its parent, AbbVie is already a Dividend Aristocrat and will soon become a Dividend King, assuming it maintains its record of increasing dividends. Its payout ratio is 47.5%, which is a great balance between sustainability and rewarding shareholders. The company pays $1.18 per share quarterly, which works out to a five percent yield annually. Investing $8,000 in AbbVie will net you just over $400 per year in cash flow ($100 per quarter.) Its beta is low as well, meaning the stock's volatility is less than the market average.

Given that Humira's 2023 patent expiration is already known, the event is priced into the stock by the market. In 2019, the firm acquired Irish pharmaceutical company Allergan for a reported $63 billion. Allergan is mostly famous for being the manufacturer of Botox. This diversifies AbbVie's product offerings.

In terms of future prospects, the company currently has over 120 clinical trials with more than 60 of these in the mid to late trial stage. AbbVie also holds several cannabis-related patents, including cannabinoids used to treat cancer, a treatment for juvenile idiopathic arthritis, and cannabis to treat skin disorders. A study by Data Bridge Market Research projects the Medical Marijuana market poised to be worth over $82 Billion by 2027. If AbbVie can capture just a fraction of the market share, this will mean great things for the company's outlook.

The next five years are being characterized as low growth for this company, but we're extremely positive on the long-term outlook with a solid 5.5% dividend in the meantime.

Chevron Corporation (NYSE:CVX)

Market Cap - $137 billion
52 week high/low - 122.94/51.60
Current yield - 6.3%
Beta - 1.26
Number of years of dividend increases - 34

Don't be fooled by the higher beta value of this stock. Chevron is a classic example of how Warren Buffett's recommendation of being greedy when others are fearful and fearful when others are greedy can make you money. The stock currently has a high beta because the oil industry and energy sector have been battered throughout 2020.

Oil prices have steadily declined, and with the current pandemic, the stock has fallen 30% this year. It has also reported a large quarterly loss in Q2 due to falling demand. However, your job isn't to think in quarters. It's to think in decades.

Rewind back to 2005, and we see that Chevron was the smallest of the U.S domestic oil producers. As of this writing, it's close to toppling ExxonMobil for the top spot. The energy sector hasn't been battered just in the markets. Public sentiment against oil producers has been turning negative as well. All around the world, governments, and people are waking up to the realities of climate change, and alternative energy use is on the rise.

However, this doesn't mean alternative energy sources are ready to replace oil. Within the next 50 years, we see oil becoming obsolete, but not within the next decade. The fundamentals of the sector remain the same. After all, it took 100 years for oil to replace coal. While the replacement process will occur quickly in the developed world, the developing world is another issue.

Even the likes of China, which is a fully developed economy, relies on oil heavily. This is also the case with other economies such as Brazil and India. As one of the world's top producers, Chevron is uniquely positioned to prosper over the next decade. The company's debt to equity ratio is just 0.25, which means it isn't heavily leveraged. It's a lean operation for an oil and gas company. The next best debt to equity ratio is Exxon with 0.38. This will stand Chevron in good stead as oil promises to be volatile for the upcoming decade.

One of the strongest points of this company is its management. They are committed to rewarding shareholders with dividends. On their Q2 earnings call, CFO Pierre Breber stated (*2Q20 Earnings Conference Call Edited Transcript, 2020*):

"All of our actions are designed consistent with our financial priorities. The first is to sustain and grow the dividend. We showed our stress test last quarter at $30 [crude oil prices] that I think was made very clear that we have the financial capability and the flexibility in our capital program, the ability to manage our costs to sustain that dividend through what is a stress test."

Chevron's management has repeatedly shown remarkable capital management in a sector that is rife with overleveraging and excessive spending. Acquisitions are commonplace in the energy sector, and companies often acquire others to present themselves as having done something. However, Chevron's management was willing to walk away from a deal in 2019 because it was deemed too expensive. They then acquired oil and gas producer Noble Energy in 2019 for what was considered a relative bargain.

As you can see from Breber's comment above, the dividend is safe until mid 2021 and has been stress tested to withstand oil prices of $30 per barrel. As of this writing, oil prices are above $40 per barrel. Given its high yield of six percent and strong company fundamentals, it's hard to find a better energy prospect than Chevron.

IBM (NYSE:IBM)

Market Cap - $99.94 billion

52 week high/low - 158.75/90.56

Current yield - 5.14%

Beta - 1.16

Number of years of dividend increases - 25

IBM is another example of a company that has been beaten down recently. Once an innovator in the technology space, it is treated as a grandfather of the industry these days. It has a market cap of close to $100 billion, which looks like pocket change compared to Apple's $2.75 trillion. From 2015 onwards, IBM's core business was beset by declining revenues and a complex management structure.

Detractors even named it International Bureaucratic Monstrosity for its complex structure. These days, IBM has moved well away from its days as a mainframe supplier to providing cloud computing, data analytics, and AI services. In line with this vision, the new CEO Arvind Krishna hails from the cloud computing division. Microsoft made a similar pivot in 2014, and over the past six years has witnessed huge growth.

Krishna's first quarter in charge was a positive one, with earnings and revenue beating analyst estimates. Cloud revenue was up 30% in the previous quarter, which continues to reinforce IBM's desire to move into the cloud computing world. Its cloud computing division now makes up 33% of overall revenues. In the next quarter, it is expected to surpass technology services as the largest revenue division for the entire company. The overall cloud computing market is valued at $1.2 trillion, with almost half of that market being a potential fit for the company's business consulting division.

IBM's cloud services are sufficiently differentiated enough from Google, Microsoft, and Amazon offerings to make an impact. 60% of their contacts are on a recurring revenue stream. Recent customer wins include Adobe, Salesforce,

SAP, Box, and Slack. All are using IBM's hybrid cloud platform to modernize mission-critical workloads.

The acquisition of Red Hat in 2019 put some strain on IBM's balance sheet. However, IBM has enough cash flow to cover the stress from it. In addition, IBM also acquired AI pioneer WDG Automation.

IBM has a proud history of increasing dividend payouts. The company kept growing dividends through the darkest days of the dotcom crash in 2000 and throughout the financial crisis of 2007-2009. We expect to see a similar story as we move forward, with a return to solid growth numbers in 2021.

We also like the makeup of the new management team, particularly with their preference for share ownership. Currently, the management team owns around 400,000 shares, which gives them a significant incentive to perform.

Another important metric is the value of share compensation relative to cash compensation. IBM's management team has share to cash compensation ratios between five and eleven, with anything over three considered significant from a "management buy-in" perspective.

Trading at just 11x forward earnings, it is a bargain when the rest of the S&P 500 is around 27x current earnings. The company has massive upside potential with its new direction. It can use its size and depth of experience to fully capitalize on future cloud computing opportunities while still offering healthy dividend payouts for income investors.

AT&T (NYSE:T)

Market Cap - $194.65 billion

52 week high/low - 39.7/26.08

Current yield - 7.07%

Beta - 0.64

Number of years of dividend increases - 35

We've highlighted the positives of AT&T previously in this book. With 170 million customers and revenues of $170 billion, it's the largest telecom operator in the world. The high yield is explained partly due to investors getting alarmed at the high levels of debt on the books and pushing the stock price lower. $152 billion is an alarming figure, but it isn't all that bad upon close inspection. This figure is 15% lower than its current book value and factors in debt following Time Warner's acquisition.

Free cash flow is projected at $23 billion, which is down from pre-pandemic levels of $29 billion. Dividend payments currently cost AT&T $14 billion annually. Assuming the company uses the remaining amount to pay down its debt at current rates, it could reduce its debt burden to $100 billion by 2025.

Buying a company with strong long-term cash flows during a time of trouble is a time-tested way to outperform. Of course, the current dividend yield is extremely enticing for investors. The financials show no indication of this being cut anytime soon.

The stock was also battered due to the company's perceived slowness to enter the streaming revolution. In fact, HBO Max was slated to release in 2018 but was delayed due to the failed DOJ suit that was brought against the company concerning its acquisition of TimeWarner. This allowed Apple and Disney to get the jump on the streaming game. However, with HBO Max now launched, we expect it to bring massive cash flow to its parent.

AT&T currently trades at just 9.3 times earnings even though the current year's earnings will be weaker due to the pandemic. We fully expect earnings to recover to their usual level as the world moves forward. The current earnings multiple is half of what it was 20 years ago. The stock is also a favorite with covered call writers, thanks to the relatively flat price movements. If you'd like to know more about covered call writing, we covered this income strategy in depth in our book *Covered Calls for Beginners.*

A low beta of 0.64 also means that it fluctuates 36% less than the rest of the market. All of this makes AT&T a great income-generating stock.

ExxonMobil (NYSE:XOM)

Market Cap - $141 billion

52 week high/low - 73.12/30.11

Current yield - 8.7%

Beta - 1.31

Number of years of dividend increases - 37

With the stock price down 40% this year, perhaps no other large cap stock has been beaten down more than Exxon. This fall culminated in the stock being removed from the Dow Jones Index after nearly 100 years. It's a spectacular fall from grace for the company, which was the largest in the world by market capitalization in 2007.

While being removed from the Dow is not a death sentence (Honeywell International, one of the largest industrial companies in the US, re-entered the index in 2020, 12 years after it was initially removed), conditions have changed. As of this writing, Tesla has a higher market capitalization than BP, Shell and Exxon combined.

The bad news doesn't end there. On a 20-year basis, Exxon stock is down 3.5%, compared to the S&P 500, which is up 130%. The COVID-19 pandemic created chaos in the oil and gas industry, with demand plummeting. This culminated in oil and gas futures going negative for the first time ever. So with all this bad news, why would we recommend Exxon? Surely the company seems doomed at this point?

For starters, bankruptcy is not on the table. A debt to equity ratio of 0.38 is much lower than its peers. For example, BP is at 1.1. Secondly, as we already noted with Chevron, oil demand will recover. It's already back up to $40/barrel from the lows we saw in April/May. Besides, with emerging markets still relying heavily on oil and gas, we don't see demand for oil disappearing anytime soon over the next decade. This prediction is backed up by the International Energy

Agency's long-term outlook despite carbon emission reductions being a global focus.

Exxon is doubling down on its core competency while its competitors like BP and Shell are moving towards a more renewable energy-focused business model. The important thing to remember is that energy shifts take decades rather than years. Oil will still be relevant for the next decade. The low stock price provides you with a great entry point.

What you may not know is that Exxon is an "integrated" oil company. It doesn't make all of its money from drilling operations. It also has refining and chemical divisions that generate cash. This sets it apart from most of its peers who primarily rely on drilling, which will have to be scaled back over the next few years.

In their Q2 earnings call, management reiterated their stance on supporting the dividend payouts while its competitors cut their payments. If its dividend payout remains rock-solid, it'll double shareholders' reinvested dividends in roughly eight years (Williams, 2020).

However, a dividend cut is possible because management also stated that it would not add more debt. This largely depends on which way oil prices go. The mass global shutdowns of March/April/May 2020 are unlikely to be repeated at such a scale, even if individual countries choose to once again go into lockdown.

Despite the perceived risks, Exxon remains a behemoth that is unlikely to go anywhere. We expect the company to provide its shareholders with steady dividend checks for the next decade at the very least.

Kinder Morgan (NYSE:KMI)

Market Cap - $28 billion
52 week high/low - 22.58/9.42
Current yield - 7.3%
Beta - 0.93
Number of years of dividend increases - 5

We're aware that we previously highlighted Kinder Morgan as an example of a dividend trap. However, bear with us because this a fantastic example of a company recognizing its own shortcomings.

Kinder Morgan is one of the largest energy infrastructure companies in North America. It owns or operates more than 83,000 miles of pipelines that transport oil, natural gas, refined petroleum products, and carbon dioxide. The company's stock was down 34% in 2020 due to lower oil and gas prices and fears that future demand for oil and gas will be less than today.

Kinder Morgan thinks this impact will only affect its 2020 earnings by about nine percent thanks to its reliance on long-term contracts (Foelber, 2020). This is because 68% of the company's earnings come from what is known as "take or pay" contracts, which are unaffected by natural gas prices.

The question of sustaining the dividend is a key one with KMI. Fortunately, smart capital management means that current levels are sustainable. The Q2 dividend payout was covered 1.7x by that quarter's earnings, showing a healthy balance sheet even amid uncertainty. During the Q2 earnings call, CEO Rich Kinder stated,

"We want adequate coverage of that dividend, and we want to make damn certain that once we do a dividend increase, that dividend increase is permanent and that we're not retracting that at some later date."

Unlike other stocks here, KMI has only increased its dividend for the past five years, after cutting it in 2015. Since then, significant management changes have been made, and in terms of dividends, the outlook has never been more positive than it is today. Although this was a short-term hit for income investors, it was the right move for long-term company sustainability, and that has been rewarded today with higher dividend yields.

2021's expansion budgets have been cut by 30%, which is expected with the current economic outlook. In our view, this shows restraint on the part of management, rather than going further into debt to fuel growth, as the company has done in the past.

The company has bought a number of Master Limited Partnerships (MLPs), and continues to be able to absorb smaller companies in its sector. If organic expansion becomes less of a possibility, then growth by acquisition is likely to become more of a factor. Kinder Morgan will be a lot more boring than it was five years ago, but that's a good thing for income investors who want a company that produces reliable cash flow and is now more focused on paying and growing its dividend.

People's United Financial Inc. (NASDAQ:PBCT)

Market Cap - $4.71 billion

52 week high/low - 17.22/9.37

Current yield - 6.6%

Beta - 1.18

Number of years of dividend increases - 49

This is a company that Warren Buffett would love: a well-run business that exercises great capital management while expanding within its circle of competence. People's United is much smaller than the other companies on this list. It isn't even a large cap. However, given its stellar performance, we're optimistic that there are great things in store for this company.

As a bit of a background, at the time of writing, we've just come out of the strongest 100-day rally in market history, with the S&P 500 up 50.8% in that time. The index now trades at a forward PE of 22.8x, over two standard deviations from the mean. This forward PE level has only been experienced around five other times in the market's history. The last time prices were this high was in 1999 before the DOTCOM crash.

One sector which didn't experience much of a rally was the banking sector. The sector has come under a lot of stress over the past six months, with large national banks bearing most of this. However, there are still many opportunities in the regional banking sector.

PBCT is based in the Northeast and controls over 400 bank branches in the region. Most importantly, the bank is diversified. No loan category makes up more than 35% of the commercial real estate portfolio and no category counts for more than 26% in the bank's equipment financing, commercial and industrial loan portfolios. This is key because it means there is no liability for a single point of failure like there would be, for example, if 90% of its loans were to the restaurant or retail industry.

The bank has no material exposure to loans in airlines, cruise lines, casinos, student loans, auto lending, or consumer credit cards - industries that are deemed to be higher risk in the currently uncertain market environment. Both Q1 and Q2 earnings were up year on year, despite uncertainty due to COVID-19. Its balance sheet is strong, with a debt-to-equity ratio of 0.31.

An important metric in the banking sector is credit rating, because this correlates with risk of bankruptcy in the long term. PBCT currently has a rating of BBB+, which roughly equates to a 0.6% chance of bankruptcy over the next 30 years. In terms of dividends, the bank returns 34% of its capital as dividends, roughly triple the S&P 500 average.

The company is still growing. It made 16 acquisitions over the past decade, which have roughly doubled its total assets to around $45 billion. Its last three acquisitions added $16 billion worth of assets to its balance sheet. PBCT continues to expand its wealth management business to keep up with increased demand from people looking for portfolio guidance in this uncertain market environment and is expanding its digital offerings to clients.

Currently the company trades at a PE of just 9.7x compared to the market average of 27x. It is also a potential acquisition target if one of the national players wants more exposure to the Northeast market. Dividends of $0.71/share will net you an annual income of $643 on a $10,000 initial investment, paid quarterly.

In short, PBCT is a great dividend player as well as a value stock to hold for the next decade (unless it gets bought out, but then you'll get a great payday to make up for it).

Now that we've covered our seven favorite dividend growth stocks, it's time to look at another sector than income investors favor, real estate.

10

OUR 2 FAVORITE REITS

"The best investment on earth is earth"

— LOUIS GLICKMAN

R eal estate is widely considered one of the best investments on the planet because land is limited and growing populations always need a place to live and work. The typical method of investing in real estate is to buy property via financing.

However, owning physical property poses a few challenges. First, it requires you to have enough money for a down payment, which can be substantial. Second, it's not a passive investment. If a pipe in your property bursts at three in the morning, you'll need to attend to it.

Real Estate Investment Trusts (REITs) provide a more comfortable alternative. For example, what if, in addition to investing in Amazon, you could also invest in Amazon's Landlord?

There are many different kinds of REITs you can invest in. Some are diversified across all forms of real estate, while others specialize in certain property types (residential, commercial, shopping centers, hospitals, raw land, etc.)

For income investors, the big benefit of REITs is that they are legally mandated to pay out 90% of their profits to shareholders, making them income-generation machines. Stag Industrial is one such REIT. They own many of the warehouses which are then leased to Amazon as they store and ship goods; because of this, the company is often referred to as "Amazon's Landlord".

Most significantly, over the past 30 years, the U.S REIT index has outperformed the S&P 500 and has posted returns of 10.6% per year on average. All of this means a well-diversified portfolio of REITs can help you achieve your income and capital gains goals.

IMPORTANT REIT METRICS

Analyzing individual REITs isn't as complicated as it seems. Here are the key metrics you need to look for when examining REITs.

Funds From Operations

Think of FFO as equivalent to the net income per share for a REIT. You can calculate FFO by adding non-cash expenses back to net income. Depreciation is a substantial non-cash expense that REITs experience. However, depreciation as an expense makes no sense when evaluating a REIT.

Accounting rules state that all assets must be depreciated. This makes sense if the asset is a physical good or a factory with a definite term of use. However, well-maintained real estate doesn't decrease in value. Instead, it appreciates. This means REITs write down perfectly good assets on their books through large depreciation expenses when, in reality, these assets are appreciating in value.

Large depreciation expenses mean that many REITS pay dividends above their net income. Don't mistake this for irresponsibility when you notice it. It's merely a quirk of how accounting works. REITs will clearly indicate their FFO numbers in their financial reports since this is a more relevant metric.

FREEMAN INCOME INVESTING RULE #5

GOOD REITs INCREASE THEIR FFO ON AN ANNUAL BASIS.

Credit Ratings

REITs make money by managing large properties and collecting rents from their tenants. Like every other real estate purchase, they finance their properties through mortgages and lines of credit. This means their credit ratings are important because it reflects the degree of confidence creditors have in the company. A high credit rating means lenders think that the REIT will repay its debts and is managing its properties well. A low credit rating implies the opposite.

Rent Collected

Ideally, REITs will be able to collect 100% of the rents they're owed from their tenants. However, we don't live in an ideal world. The pandemic shined a light on which REITs were efficient at collecting rents and which ones weren't. REITs manage hundreds of properties, and it's impossible to collect 100% of the rent all the time.

However, good REITs attract high quality tenants who are less affected by sudden disruptions. During the lockdown period, we paid particular attention to the rent collected by REITs. Some low quality companies weren't able to collect even half of the rents they were owed. Others, high quality ones, were relatively unaffected.

Here are the two best REITs that we have identified.

Realty Income (NYSE:O) has reliably paid monthly dividends for more than 25 years now, making it the perfect stock for retirement investors. It's also one of the few monthly dividend payers that are worthy investments. The company leases single-tenant properties to retailers that are largely immune to e-commerce headwinds and that are recession-resistant. These are businesses such as convenience stores, drugstores, dollar stores, and others that do well in all economic conditions.

The company currently has a $28 billion market capitalization. Typically, tenants sign long-term net leases, which require them to pay for property taxes, insurance, and maintenance. This shifts the variable costs of the property to the tenant (Frankel, 2020).

Realty Income has declared over 600 consecutive monthly dividend payments without interruption and has increased its dividend 107 times since its initial public offering in 1994. It has a 20-year annualized return of 15.3%.

To put this kind of performance in perspective, if you invest $5,000 per year and your money grows at this rate (15.3%), you'll end up with $530,000 after 20 years. After 30 years that's $2.3 million. You could become a real estate million-aire without owning any real estate!

At the same time, the company's beta is just 0.4. This means not only did Realty Income thus easily outperform the broad market, but it also did so while being a less risky/less volatile investment at the same time. In the 2020 second quarter, adjusted funds from operations per share increased 4.9% to $0.86 year-over-year (*Realty Income Announces Operating Results For Second Quarter And First Six Months Of 2020*, 2020). Realty Income collected 86.5% of contractual rent across the total portfolio. AFFO (FFO minus revenue accruals & capital expenses) growth was due to a combination of rental increases at existing prop-erties, as well as contributions from new properties.

Average lease term remaining is a healthy nine years, which means there aren't likely to be many cash flow shocks in the near future if tenants do not renew their leases. It's one of the two REITs which is both A rated by Moody's and has had increasing dividend payouts for the past 25 years. A strong management team is committed to the cause, and insider buying numbers continue to increase year on year.

While other REITs have been struggling to collect rent and maintain their dividends, **W.P. Carey (NYSE:WPC)** has sailed through the COVID-19 downturn without breaking a sweat.

And while other REITs cut dividends during the pandemic, W.P. Carey was one of the few to raise dividends (as did Realty Income). The company collected 97% of rents in April, the highest of any major REIT. Meanwhile, W.P. Carey's closest competitor, National Retail Properties, collected just 52%.

The reason for this outperformance was W.P. Carey's diversified portfolio. It currently owns a portfolio composed of 24% industrials, 23% office space, 22% warehouse, and 17% retail. Like Realty Income, it's a net-lease provider. It buys properties from companies and then instantly rents them back to the seller with a long-term lease. The seller, meanwhile, is responsible for most of the operating costs of the property they occupy. It's really more of a financial transaction, with the seller raising cash it can put to better use elsewhere. And since the lessee is responsible for most of the operating costs, W.P.Carey just gets to sit back and collect the rent.

The company is more active than other REITs and is continuously looking for opportunities to expand its portfolio across the world. In the previous decade, management believed US retail space was overvalued, so they focused more on Europe which now generates around a third of the company's rents. This gives them good protection from potential US civil unrest. They're also targeting industrial, and warehouse sectors, which they foresee will not be as affected by a post-COVID landscape.

The REIT boasts a solid 5.9% dividend yield with an annual payout of $4.17 per share, paid quarterly. It's an ideal stock to own as a hedge against another recession. If the company can still collect 97% of its rents during the biggest mass layoff in US history, that bodes well for future uncertainty. We're positive that it's strong enough to weather another storm in the long run though.

Note that we also included two other single industry-focused REITs with fantastic long-term outlook in our first book *The 8 Step Beginner's Guide to Value Investing.*

PRIVATE REITS

These days you also have the opportunity to invest in private REITs. These REITs aren't traded on the stock exchange, as their names imply. In the past, only accredited investors (those who are worth at least $1 million) could invest in them, and these instruments had high investment minimums.

However in the past decade, private REITs have become extremely popular, and you'll hear of them being also pushed as "crowdfunded REITs", with one of the more prominent examples being Cardone Capital, run by entrepreneur and YouTube influencer Grant Cardone.

When you buy a private REIT, you're buying units in the fund directly from the company. There are no shares since these companies are not publicly traded. If you wish to sell your units, you'll have to sell them to other investors or back to the REIT itself. This makes it tough to exit your investment. However, private REITs tend to have a few advantages over the average public REIT.

They pay a much higher yield for starters while only requiring a $1,000 minimum investment (on average.) Streitwise, for example, pays 9.75% per year, and you can invest in them through your IRA account. However, there are some catches you must keep in mind before investing in a private REIT.

Your money is being placed in a private fund, which means you'll have to do as the fund manager says. Typically, REIT fund managers impose lockup periods. A lockup is a phenomenon borrowed from the hedge fund world where investors have to keep their money in the fund for a certain period of time before they're allowed to withdraw it. The typical lockup lasts for around six months, but some private REITs have lockups that are as long as a year.

Many funds also impose redemption fees. For example, private REIT Upside Avenue charges two percent early withdrawal fees in the second year and a one percent fee in the third. This fee is referred to as "early withdrawal" since the fund manager expects investors to remain in the fund for the fund's entire lifespan. Each fund is typically tied to a single property, and investors earn returns directly from the rents and capital gains that the property experiences.

Most REITs can last for as long as a decade and might impose a minimum investment period of five years. Understand that the lockup is different from the minimum investment. During the lockup period, you won't have access to your funds, no matter what.

The bad news doesn't end there, though. According to an article by Michael Finke, a 2014 report by an independent REIT rating publication called Green Street Advisors concluded that privately held REITs underperformed publicly traded REITs by about 3.6 percentage points per year (Finke, 2020).

For this reason, as well as the ones listed above, we recommend you stay away from private REITs. The regular income investor can get just as good results with larger public REITs like Realty Income and W.P. Carey.

11

PARTNERSHIPS - THE UNDERGROUND SECRET TO MASSIVE DIVIDENDS

Master limited partnerships or MLPs have long been a source of great dividends for wealthy investors. These legal structures used to be employed by companies to help pay their owners' massive dividends and avoid the resulting tax burden.

But now with many MLPs trading on public stock exchanges, it's now easy for regular income investors to realize the benefits of these vehicles.

First, what is an MLP? An MLP is a partnership that derives its income from a resource. To qualify as an MLP, the partnership must derive at least 90% of its income from either commodity operations, natural resources, or real estate (McClay, 2020). MLPs are usually founded by parent firms and their largest shareholders often own stock in the parent company as well. Thus the biggest shareholders of the MLP are traditionally the management team of the parent company.

Partnerships are taxed differently from other legal structures. In the past, many MLPs were used to reduce taxes on the primary companies they were tied to. The partners in an MLP would charge these firms massive fees, on paper. Thus, the firms would get to declare a loss while the partners of the MLP would with-draw their profits as dividends.

Another way to reduce taxes on the MLP's payouts would be to declare these dividends as ROC or return of capital. This is why the IRS treats ROC as a reduction of the cost basis of your investment. We'll discuss what this means shortly. For now, let's dive deeper into MLPs and look at how you can put them to use.

HOW MLPS WORK

MLPs are income-generation machines, and best of all, you can buy shares in them on a public stock exchange. As we just outlined, there are many companies that use MLPs to create losses on their books. Large public companies don't do this anymore due to the reputational damage they'd sustain. However, many smaller MLPs and firms continue to rely on this tactic and you ought to watch out for them.

These partnerships have gained a poor reputation amongst the online invest-ment community, but as we've repeatedly highlighted so far, this doesn't mean MLPs are a bad investment. You need to conduct your research into them before investing. Not every MLP is the same.

For example, MLPs are used by oil and gas companies to hold assets such as tankers and pipelines. These assets usually depreciate and decrease the parent company's earnings. To remove this burden from their books, companies offload them onto an MLP, pay fees to the MLP, and use that to offset the depreciation expense. The result is two profitable companies, with the MLP paying massive dividends to its partners (shareholders).

Given the fact that MLPs operate in the energy and natural resources field, you'd be right to worry about exposure to commodity price fluctuations. However, most MLPs are structured to merely hold assets and earn fees based on the volume of the resource that flows through them.

There is some jargon you need to learn before investing in MLPs. Natural resources companies typically divide their operations into three segments: upstream, midstream, and downstream.

Upstream refers to operations and earnings that are generated early in the resource extraction process. For example, exploration and drilling are considered upstream activities.

Midstream typically includes processing, storage, and marketing of the resource. Most MLPs are midstream operations. For example, Energy Transfer Partners is a midstream natural gas MLP that earns fees and pays dividends based on the volume of natural gas that flows through the pipelines it owns.

Downstream deals with all post-production activities. For example, refining crude to produce gasoline and other products is downstream activity. Upstream and downstream operations are exposed to commodity prices, but midstream operations typically aren't. The fees that a midstream MLP generates are tied to the volume of products in its storage facilities.

Upstream and downstream MLPs exist, and they do contain exposure to resource prices. Therefore for the safety of your income stream, we recommend you stick to midstream MLPs.

Taxes

No discussion of MLPs is complete without diving into how they're taxed. There's a lot of misrepresentation when it comes to the topic. MLPs are often marketed as tax-deferred entities, and this isn't strictly true. The tax implications of owning an MLP depend on the MLP itself. The matter of taxation hinges on the type of payouts that the MLP makes to its shareholders.

Dividends are usually taxed as ordinary income and treated the same as the salary you receive from your employer. This means you pay taxes at your marginal income tax rate. However, MLP dividends can be classified as ROC as we mentioned previously. ROC payments aren't taxed since they reduce your cost basis in the investment.

For example, if you bought an MLP for $100 and received $10 back as ROC, the IRS will treat your investment as if you bought it for $90 (100-10). Therefore, you won't pay taxes on the dividend payment you received.

However, you will pay taxes when you sell your investment. Let's say you sell your MLP shares after you receive the $10 dividend payment. Let's also assume that the market price of the shares of the MLP is $110. Since you bought it for $100 and are selling it for $110, your capital gains on the investment are $10 right? Wrong. Remember that the dividend reduces your cost basis. This means your effective purchase price is $90. Your capital gains are therefore $20 from the investment.

The IRS treats Capital gains taxes as two separate categories, short or long-term. We'll discuss this in more detail in the chapter on taxes. For now, understand that long-term capital gains taxes are a lot lower than short-term ones.

Over time, it is possible for your cost basis in the MLP to reduce to zero. Once this happens, you'll pay long-term capital gains taxes on your dividend payment. Remember that the ROC classification of MLP dividends depends on the MLP itself. There are MLPs that classify their payments as ordinary dividend income. These payments won't be treated as ROC. You'll need to read the annual filings of the MLP and do your research to figure out how the dividend payments are classified.

One of the biggest perceived drawbacks of investing in MLPs is the unwieldy tax form that accompanies them. Typically, you'll receive a 1099 form when investing in dividend-paying instruments. However, an investment in an MLP is treated as though you are investing in a partnership, and this means you'll receive the K-1 form. This form has acquired a notorious reputation, and many income investors shy away from MLPs because they consider it too painful to deal with.

While the K-1 isn't as straightforward as a 1099, handling it is as simple as passing it on to an accountant who'll figure it out for you. The K-1 will mention the portion of dividend payments that are ROC, ordinary income, and capital gains. Your accountant will need to keep track of your adjusted cost basis over time. When you sell your investment, they'll probably ask you to furnish them with your prior K-1s to verify your cost basis for tax purposes.

The great thing about ROC is that it works very well if you hold onto your investment indefinitely. Let's say you buy an MLP for $100 and receive $10 as dividends every year. Within ten years, your cost basis is zero, and you'll pay long-term capital gains taxes on dividends you'll receive from that point on. However, if you never sell your MLP investment, you'll never pay taxes on the $100 you received as dividends.

What's more, when you pass away, you can transfer your MLP shares to your heirs. Their cost basis is adjusted to the stock price on the day of your passing. This resets the ROC clock and once again, they'll enjoy the advantages of deferred taxes until their cost basis resets to zero.

Disadvantages of MLPs

Like with everything else, MLPs have certain disadvantages. For starters, the K-1 form poses a few challenges. This isn't to do with the way the form is treated. Rather, it usually arrives late and close to the filing deadline. In some cases, you might receive it after the deadline, and you'll need to file for an extension.

The way the MLP operates can also pose challenges to your accountant. If an MLP operates in multiple states, you might need to file separate returns with each state and will pay taxes according to the K-1. This is a headache for your accountant to deal with. Additionally, some accountants will charge you extra fees for filing a form in each state. This is something to address with your accountant *before* you begin investing in MLPs. You also can't deal with MLP taxation by yourself unless you happen to be an accountant. For some investors, the hassle of dealing with all of this for a few additional points of yield isn't worth it.

Speaking of yield, many MLPs pay high yields, greater than eight percent per year. Because of this attractive headline figure, there is much unscrupulous marketing surrounding a few of them, so you need to be careful about evaluating the company. Like regular stocks, don't invest in an MLP solely for the yield since this will only lead you to yield traps. You'll need to evaluate them as you would any individual stock or fund.

An option you can choose to avoid the K-1 is to invest in mutual funds or ETFs that invest in MLPs. This way, you'll receive the 1099 form at the end of the year while the fund deals with the K-1. However, keep in mind that there aren't many low-cost ETFs that invest in MLPs. They're a more complicated investment than just buying stocks, and as a result, active management is required. The fees associated will, therefore be higher. You'll need to evaluate how much you think the reduced tax filing burden is worth before investing in a managed fund.

Given their relatively high yields, MLPs don't provide the best capital appreciation. To understand this, we need to look at how companies use them. Most of them are structured as special vehicles used to offset losses resulting from regular operations. For example, an upstream MLP is used to capture the losses associated with the surveying and exploration process. The MLP draws depreciation and capital losses away from the parent company and boosts the latter's profits. While such an MLP might pay high dividends, its stock price might decline over time.

Midstream MLPs are far more stable, but again, they're asset vehicles. Once the assets have been written down, the parent company might decide to create another MLP and might wind the existing one down. This means you'll have to find another vehicle to fill that dividend income hole. This isn't a disadvantage per se. It's just that you need to be aware of how MLPs work and how parent companies treat them.

This is why it's important to invest in the right structures, backed by reputable companies. Any high-yielding MLP won't work since the structure might not be beneficial to you. You'll see some MLPs yielding 25% annually. These are yield traps and have such high payouts due to declining share prices, not just because of increased dividends.

The annual filings are the best way of figuring out what an MLP is all about. Some of the standard shenanigans that occur with low quality MLPs are asset maneuvering and yield inflation. Asset maneuvering refers to when a parent company will suddenly decide to transfer all of an MLPs assets to another vehicle without notice. Technically speaking, every MLP investment runs this risk. However, you want to watch for the reputation of the parent company.

Yield inflation occurs when a company aggressively pushes its high yield nature on investors. Such companies are usually looking to dump their stock onto new shareholders while the older ones exit. Look for a breakdown of their dividends. Typically, most of their payments will be ordinary income, which means you won't realize any tax advantages. Combine this with a falling stock price, and you'll end up having your money dwindle quickly. As a rule of thumb, the easier it is for you to understand how the MLP works and generates money, the better your investment will be.

TWO MLPS WORTH INVESTING IN

Here are two high quality MLPs that we believe are worth an investment.

Enterprise Products Partners (NYSE:EPD)

Stock Price: $20.21
52 week high/low: $29.22/$10.27
Market Cap: $44.8 Billion
Dividend yield: 10%
Number of consecutive years with dividend increases: 23

Enterprise Products Partners is a high income instrument that boasts a stable 10% yield. Stable and 10% yield might sound like an oxymoron, but thanks to the MLP structure, it's not just a possibility; it's a reality.

This midstream MLP is a play on the energy sector. While the sector has been hammered in 2020, there are still a number of great opportunities for investors looking for reliable income streams. There is a misconception in this sector that all "oil companies" make their money from drilling expeditions, which leaves them highly exposed to falling oil prices. This isn't true. As we explained previously, upstream, downstream, and midstream operations are very different.

Enterprise operates in the midstream segment. Upstream companies that drill for oil and gas (like ConocoPhillips or Schlumberger) suffer from volatile commodity prices that don't dictate Enterprise's top or bottom-line results. Downstream companies (like Marathon Oil) refine oil and gas or make chemicals. For these companies, earnings are driven by the difference between input costs and the final sale price of its products.

By operating pipelines and transportation services, Enterprise is what you might think of as a "toll booth" stock in that it collects fees regardless of oil prices. This makes it a fundamentally safer business model than that of upstream or downstream companies. To illustrate this, Enterprise's earnings rose during Q1 2020, when drilling companies were suffering. Best of all, it has covered its distributions by 1.6x in Q1, meaning that it isn't paying out shareholders with debt.

EPD does have its share of competitors. Enbridge is often referred to as EPD's biggest competitor. However, the biggest drawback with Enbridge is that it is a Canadian company, therefore the dividend is paid in Canadian dollars, which leaves you exposed to foreign exchange risk, and you may not be able to exercise DRIPs on your broker platform. Besides, EPD has a more conservative balance sheet with Debt to EBITDA of 3.7 vs. 7 for Enbridge. With dividends at $1.78 per share this represents around a 10% yield based on current market prices. Dividends are paid quarterly.

Slow growth is expected in the next 5-10 years, but this should be considered a pure income play with a 8-10% distribution from a solid company - near impossible to find anywhere on the market.

Brookfield Renewable Energy (NYSE:BEP)

Stock Price: $62.53

52 week high/low: $64.94/$30.09

Market cap: $11.5 Billion

Dividend yield - 3.1%

Number of consecutive years with dividend increases: 7

Brookfield is the new renewable energy kid on the block and competes against the legacy oil industry. A huge run from March lows has now pushed the stock above February highs again, meaning over the past three years, it has nearly tripled the returns of the S&P 500. Despite this growth, it still has a healthy distribution coverage of 1.4x. Management targets between 1.4 and 1.67x distribution coverage as a long-term sustainable level.

The great thing about Brookfield is that it isn't just a pure income play. You can expect significant capital gains growth in addition to earning a steady dividend income. When it comes to the stock market valuing a company, there are a couple of ways in which it might happen.

First, the market might get caught up with the hype surrounding a company and send its stock to dizzying heights. Nio, dubbed "The Tesla of China" is a good example of this. The company manufactures just 16,000 vehicles per quarter, each one at a loss, and yet it currently has a higher market cap than Honda and Ford. Nio is an example of how emotions often drive lofty valuations in stocks.

Brookfield is an example of the second way in which the markets value companies. Its valuation is backed by solid financials instead of hype. The company owns and operates a portfolio of renewable power generating facilities including 193 hydroelectric generating stations, 11 wind facilities and two natural gas-fired plants in the USA, Canada, and Brazil.

The demand for electricity is consistent compared to oil or gas, which gives the company predictable, reliable cash flow. It sells the bulk of its power through long-term fixed contracts, so its income is not directly dependent on plant output. Brookfield acquired TerraForm Power in July, and when combined they will be one of the largest renewable energy companies on earth with a capacity of 19,000 MW.

Management predicts that cash flow will grow by 6-11% over the next two years, despite the current worldwide economic situation. Including growth, Brookfield shareholders are looking at a 10-14% annual growth rate, which is fantastic for a company with high distributions as well. What's more, distribution payouts have increased by over 300% in the past decade. Management aims to increase payouts by eight percent a year going forward.

We'd like to mention that in your brokerage account, you may see two companies trading under similar names: Brookfield Renewable Inc. and Brookfield Renewable Partners L.P. The MLP is Brookfield Renewable Partners L.P. and trades under the symbol (NYSE:BEP).

FREEMAN INCOME INVESTING RULE #6

STICK TO MIDSTREAM MLPs IF YOU DON'T
WANT TO BE EXPOSED TO FLUCTUATIONS
IN COMMODITY PRICES

Now we've covered stocks, REITs and MLPs. It's time to look at the "cherry on the cake" of income investing.

12

CLOSED-END BOND FUNDS – AN INCOME INVESTOR'S DREAM

Y ou've already read that we aren't the biggest fans of mutual funds or managed funds, because while they target outperformance, they rarely ever achieve it. If you want to stick to funds rather than individual stocks, targeting the market average and minimizing expenses is the way to go. However, there is one significant exception to this, namely the Closed End Bond Fund or CEF.

Most mutual funds suffer from underperformance due to their structure. The average mutual fund manager needs to be a marketing machine while figuring out how to invest the money they're charged with. The stock market allows people to buy new units in the fund, and this means they need to constantly find ways to make more money with an increasing capital base. This leads to less than optimal asset allocation and underperformance is the result.

Not every mutual fund is set up to fail like this. The fact that you can always buy new units of a mutual fund means that it is open-ended. However, there are also closed-ended mutual funds. These funds raise a fixed amount of capital from investors and then close the fund to new subscriptions. Their shares trade on the market, but since you'll be buying shares from existing investors, their capital base doesn't increase. This means the fund manager can concentrate on allocating capital to the best of their abilities, and not worrying about finding new places to park money.

You'll notice that we've mentioned bonds in the title of this chapter. As you grow older, your investment focus will naturally shift towards income generation instead of capital gains. We've already mentioned the 60/40 and "subtract your age from 100" rule of thumb asset allocation calculations that most financial advisors resort to. Despite the fallacy of that method, there's no denying that as you get older, you need to focus more of your investments toward bonds or fixed income assets.

Closed-ended bond funds are a great choice since they're both actively managed, and their pricing structure often results in bargains. Why are these two such huge advantages?

FUND STRUCTURES

Why is active management a good thing in this case? We've highlighted previously that passively managed funds do better in the long run. However, bonds are an exception to the rule. The reason being that bonds are more complex than stocks and require active management.

Bonds are primarily traded by institutions. Despite the bond market's size being much bigger than the stock market, almost $40 trillion compared to $15 trillion for stocks, the number of traders and participants in the market is less than the stock market. However, thanks to every participant being an institution of some kind, the average trade size runs well into the hundreds of millions of dollars.

The other thing to note about bond markets is that there are no insider trading laws or other investor protections like those in the stock market. The financial authorities figure that everyone can take care of themselves and know what they're doing when trading bonds. This makes it crucial for a money manager to be on top of things and react quickly when they need to. This is also why active management is much more preferable in the bond market.

The second reason for investing in closed-ended bond funds is the price structure. This is unique to closed-ended funds in the investment world. Every fund (whether passive or active) has a net asset value or NAV that indicates the total monetary value of the units the fund holds.

For example, if a fund raises $100 million from investors and invests it in securities that rise to $200 million, the fund's NAV is $200 million. You would expect that the NAV divided by the number of units would be equal to the price at which the fund trades in the market.

This is how mutual funds work. Their NAV is calculated at the end of a market day and that is the price at which investors can buy or sell the fund's units. With closed-ended funds this doesn't happen. Their prices fluctuate during the day as stocks and ETFs do. This means their unit prices won't always match their NAV. Some funds trade at a premium to NAV and some at a discount.

You might think that the ones trading at a premium are high quality and the discounted ones are of a low quality. However, this isn't the case. There are many reasons why a fund can trade at a discount, such as market perception, bad analyst ratings, and current events. Like any company whose stock price can get depressed for various reasons, closed-ended funds' unit prices are subject to emotions of short-term market participants.

This is an opportunity for you to jump in and earn a high yield on your investment. A fund that would normally yield five percent to NAV might be yielding 10% or more thanks to the discount at which it trades. Remember that the fund does not issue new units to the market. You'll be buying from existing investors. This is often a reason for steep discounts in prices.

The reason is that smaller closed-ended funds suffer from a lack of liquidity. If existing investors in a fund don't wish to sell, and if the fund isn't issuing new units to bring new investors on board, the market for selling existing units is pretty small. This leads to a price discount. Liquidity is an important factor when investing, but if your outlook is longer than a decade, you won't have to worry about it. This is because you'll capture the capital appreciation over time, and even if you sell at a discount to NAV in the future, you'll still be selling at a higher price than what you bought the fund for.

Many income investors buy closed-ended funds with the hope of trying to capture the price rise from a discount to NAV. This is the wrong way to do things. It's a lot like buying a stock before it goes ex-dividend since you know the dividend is on the way. It's a short-term method of trying to make money, and it doesn't work. You can't control the discount at which the fund's units sell. Instead, understand what the fund does and seek to remain invested over the long term. The discount merely gets you a good entry into a great asset.

Since they seek outperformance, closed-ended funds charge high performance and management fees. You won't be charged loading fees though. You're buying their shares in the market and this means the manager doesn't have to deal with new funds to allocate. However, the fact that the investor base is small results in funds charging higher than normal fees. Some of the best closed-ended funds charge as much as 1.7% in annual fees, which is a high hurdle (*What to know about buying closed-end funds at a discount*, 2020).

Bond funds charge lower fees since their capital returns are lower. However, these fees are still greater than what you can expect with a passively managed ETF. The idea is to offset the higher fees against the promise of outperformance. Some bond funds have returned as much as stock funds, though. A shining example is the AllianceBernstein High Income Fund that has returned 10.9% annually over the past 25 years. The fund currently holds over 1,163 corporate bonds.

OTHER ADVANTAGES

Closed-ended funds are treated differently by the SEC than mutual funds. Mutual funds operate in a strict regulatory environment and cannot deviate from their guidelines no matter what. The same isn't true of closed-ended funds. This is not to say that they have a hedge fund-like independence. It's just that they have a more comprehensive array of choices for assets they can invest in.

For example, closed-ended funds can invest in below investment grade bonds. Each bond is given a grade or credit rating by Standard & Poor's and Moody's, the two ratings agencies. The rating scale that each agency uses is slightly different, but generally speaking, anything below an A grade is considered less than investment worthy.

The thing about these riskier bonds is that this is where true bargains are found. The moment a bond is downgraded to less than investment worthy, its price plummets, and its yield rises.

As we mentioned earlier, bond prices are quoted in percentages, so let's look at an example of this. Let's say a bond was trading at 100 (100% of its face value) and was yielding two percent. Once the downgrade hits, its price could plummet to 60 or 50. If it falls to 50, the yield on the bond is now four percent.

There is the risk of default, but this is why you need an active manager to step in and assess opportunities. We should also note a big difference between a bond rated below investment grade and junk bonds. For example, a bond rated BBB would be considered below investment grade, but above junk bond grade. Anything below a B rating is considered junk.

When investing in closed-ended funds, pay attention to the issuer. Here are some of the fund issuers in the market who have the best track record:

- AllianceBernstein
- PIMCO
- Nuveen
- DoubleLine

WHAT TO LOOK FOR IN A BOND CEF

So what should you look for when choosing a closed-ended fund to invest in? For starters you should stick to funds that are trading at a discount to NAV. There's no specific number that you should look for. Obviously the deeper the discount, the greater your yield will be. You'll also be potentially locking in capital gains equal to the discount in case the fund rises to par value. However, as we previously mentioned, this shouldn't be your primary goal.

You can check fund discounts at https://www.cefchannel.com/screens/discount-to-nav/. You'll find quite a few high quality funds trading at a discount. For example, Calamos Dynamic Convertible and Income Fund (CCD) CEF has returned 19.39% YTD, has an annual distribution of 8.87%, and still trades for an 11.37% discount to NAV. Don't be swayed into buying funds that trade for a premium. There's less upside to these investments than there is in stocks. Income is what you should be after. This is why choosing a high quality fund with the biggest discount works best.

A larger discount also means you'll have the fund's management fee paid for. For example, if you buy a fund that charges one percent management fees at a five percent discount, you're still ahead after fees. Since income is your primary goal, you want to look for funds that consist of BB or BBB grade bonds. These bonds are below investment grade, but they are above the junk category. Some of them might default, but the majority of them will recover their value. Generally, these bonds trade between 70 and 90 (remember bonds prices are quoted as a percentage of their face value). Their yields aren't as high as lower-rated bonds, but they're in a sweet spot in terms of safety and yield.

You can find a fund's portfolio composition on its web page or in its prospectus. You also want to invest in funds that own bonds in stable markets. While emerging markets (countries with faster economic growth than developed countries like the US or Japan) are sexy investments, they aren't the most stable. Putting money in emerging market bonds isn't all that different from speculating in those stock markets. Stay away from taking on such risk.

Pay attention to the fund manager. The longer their track record is, the better. The issuers we highlighted previously hire excellent managers with great pedigrees. At the very least, you want a manager who has a track record that spans ten years. Check to see if the fund has outperformed its benchmark. The longer the outperformance, the better. The best sign of a good manager is someone who invests their own money into the fund.

A good example of a fund that ticks all of these boxes is the AllianceBernstein Global High Income Fund. The fund has a 10.79% annualized return over 22 years ($10,000 invested in 1998 would be worth $74,222 today). The same investment in the S&P 500 over the same time period would be worth $26,283. It has significant insider ownership as well, which makes it extremely attractive.

This fund is also a good example of how a discount can compensate for high fees. Currently, there's a 1.05% fee, but it trades at a 13% discount, so you're paying 87 cents on the dollar. That fully covers your fee, making the management essentially free. The fund currently holds 65% of its bonds in the US, with no other country making up more than five percent. 98% of its exposure in USD, so there's no foreign exchange risk. Best of all, its yield is 6.38% and is distributed monthly.

FREEMAN INCOME INVESTING RULE #7

IF YOU BUY A CEF FOR A DISCOUNT TO NAV, THEN YOU ARE ESSENTIALLY GETTING ACTIVE MANAGEMENT FOR FREE.

THE 3 BEST DIVIDEND ETFS FOR HANDS-OFF INVESTORS

While closed-ended bond funds are a good investment choice, they do come with risks. Outperformance isn't guaranteed, after all. If you're someone who wants income but is conservative when it comes to investing, dividend ETFs are a good option. While your yields will be lower, they'll be pretty stable. Like with everything else, there's a tradeoff between safety and yield.

THE BEST LOW-FEE ETF ISSUER

The best low-fee dividend ETFs are issued by the Vanguard Group. With this in mind, here are three dividend ETFs that have conservative strategies and yield a good amount of cash.

Vanguard Dividend Appreciation ETF (NASDAQ:VIG)

This is a popular ETF that tracks the Dividend Achievers index. Because the fund incurs costs when buying and selling securities in the index, it trails the index by a negligible amount. It consists of 182 companies that have increased dividend payouts for at least the past ten years.

The Dividend Achievers index is different from the Aristocrats and the Kings index in that it prioritizes capital gains along with income generation. Since companies need to have paid dividends for just ten years in a row, most companies in the index have a history of capital appreciation.

For example, VIG's biggest holdings are currently Microsoft, Visa, and Procter & Gamble. Microsoft has been one of the stock market's best performers over the past decade and has led the way with its massive capital gains. Visa has been a huge beneficiary of the pandemic, even if it has stayed away from the headlines that other tech companies have garnered. Procter & Gamble is an example of a stable dividend-paying stock that won't witness much capital appreciation but will provide steady income flow.

Some of the fund's other major holdings include Walmart, McDonald's, and Johnson & Johnson. With these three holdings, Walmart is an example of a company that has been stable in terms of both growth and dividend payouts.

It's no surprise that VIG as a fund has achieved stellar performance. It has returned 350% over a 10-year period. $10,000 invested in the fund a decade ago would have turned into $35,000 by now.

Best of all, VIG charges a low fee of just 0.06% per year. This is fantastic compared to mutual funds that charge upwards of one percent per year or some closed-ended bond funds that charge three percent or higher. The dividend yield is around 1.8%, which might sound low compared to some of the other options we've highlighted so far in this book. However, you are making up for it with higher growth rates from companies like Microsoft.

VIG is best suited if you're not looking for the highest dividend yields but want capital appreciation to balance it out. Your investment principal will be safe with VIG for the long term and you'll manage to earn steady dividend payouts as well. DRIP these payouts back into the fund and you'll grow your capital significantly.

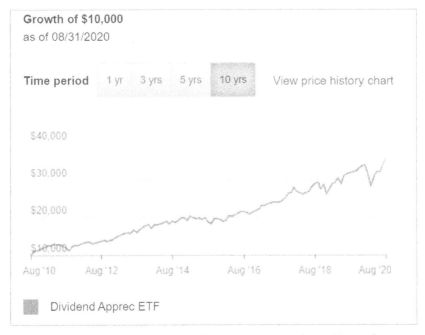

Growth of $10,000
as of 08/31/2020

Time period | 1 yr | 3 yrs | 5 yrs | 10 yrs | View price history chart

Dividend Apprec ETF

Figure 11: VIG 10 Year Performance from August 2010-2020 (Source: Vanguard)

Vanguard High Dividend Yield ETF (VYM)

Vanguard describes VYM as a high yield ETF. To this effect, the ETF tracks the FTSE High Dividend Yield Index. This index isn't as widely followed as the Dividend Achievers index, but it is a valid and thoroughly researched index nonetheless. VYM holds 426 dividend-paying companies across all industries. Currently, financials and healthcare account for the largest holdings.

Its biggest holdings are Johnson & Johnson, Procter & Gamble, and JPMorgan Chase. These companies offer a lot of stability coupled with reliable dividend payments. Other portfolio holdings include AT&T and Intel for some higher yields. Despite the high yield moniker attached to the fund, its holdings aren't exactly risky. It invests mostly in large cap companies, which means its payouts are stable.

Not only are payouts stable, the yield is a lot higher as well. VIG yields less than two percent, but VYM currently yields 3.59%. Its expense ratio is the same as

VIG, coming in at 0.06%. While it is slightly more volatile than VIG, it is still less volatile than the S&P 500. This makes it an excellent choice for conservative investors.

Keep in mind that despite the low volatility, it's still a riskier investment compared to VIG. Again, the higher yield implies more risk and reward.

Figure 12: VYM 10 Year Performance from August 2010-2020 (Source: Vanguard)

Vanguard Long-Term Treasury ETF (VGLT)

VGLT is primarily a bond ETF, specifically a US Treasury Bond ETF. The fund aims to provide stable dividend income at sustainable yields. It's extremely useful for long-term treasury exposure. 99.9% of the holdings are in US government treasuries with a weighted average of 10-25 year maturity. This is a great choice for older investors looking for additional stability in their portfolio.

VGLT currently yields 1.39%, but this is offset because it performs well in volatile market environments when stocks are falling. This is because bonds naturally become a safe haven when stocks are in turbulent waters.

Between March and September 2020, VGLT returned 25.38% compared to 6% for the S&P 500 on a YTD basis. However, the ETF underperforms during growth markets as we experienced from 2011-2020.

VGLT has monthly distributions of $0.14 per share (roughly a two percent annual yield), which is great if you want more frequent payouts. Its expense ratio is just 0.05% as compared to similar funds that charge anywhere from 0.07% up to 1%.

Vanguard places this fund squarely in the middle in terms of risk versus reward, with the previous two funds a rung above in terms of risk. This is primarily because of the bond concentration in the fund's portfolio.

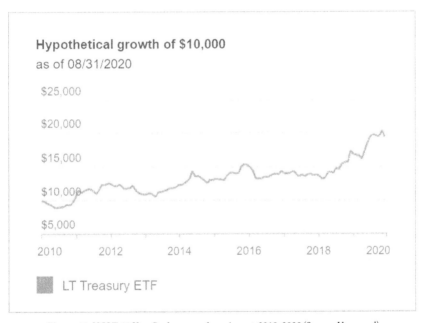

Figure 13: *VGLT 10 Year Performance from August 2010-2020 (Source: Vanguard)*

FREEMAN INCOME INVESTING RULE #8

IF YOU CAN'T (OR DON'T WANT TO) DEDICATE 30 MINUTES A DAY TO YOUR INVESTMENTS, THEN PASSIVE INVESTING WITH ETFs IS A SUPERIOR APPROACH

14

TAX IMPLICATIONS OF DIVIDENDS

Earning steady income through dividends is great, but you have to take taxes into account. Many income-seeking investors get confused by how the IRS handles taxes, and in this chapter we'll be diving deep into this topic. Don't worry though. You don't need an accounting degree to understand all of this.

We'd also like to mention that given our audience's demographics, we'll be dealing primarily with the way the US government handles dividend taxation. For our readers outside the US, be sure to check your country's laws with a qualified tax professional.

To address the biggest question you might have, the majority of dividend taxation is fairly simple to understand. The most complex taxation requirements concern MLPs as we've discussed already. The average income investor will receive the Form 1099-DIV from their broker and will simply have to input the numbers on this form into their tax return software. Popular DIY tax software like QuickBooks, H&R Block and TurboTax have instructions on their website for how to enter information from your 1099-DIV form into your standard 1040 Tax Return form.

If there's no complexity in terms of filing, why should you pay attention to taxation? Simply put, it has implications for the way you choose to invest your money. Some high yield investments might not be suited for you thanks to the way they're taxed, while lower yield instruments might work better.

Before we dive into dividend taxation, we'd like to mention that you should take full advantage of all the tax perks you're provided. If you have a retirement account or multiple accounts with employer matching, you must take advantage of this. The dividends you earn in these accounts will not be taxed until you withdraw your capital at the age of 59 and a half.

While the topic of retirement accounts is beyond the scope of this book, we'd like to merely mention that the tax deferment qualities of these accounts allow you to compound your dividend income tax-free. If you elect to DRIP your dividends, then your compounding is both automatic and tax-free.

The flip side is that you can't withdraw this money without incurring penalties before the age of 59½. However, as long as you maximize your contributions into all of your retirement accounts and manage your expenses properly, you'll find that you won't need to touch your retirement nest egg. Having covered all of that, let's look at how dividends are taxed.

DIVIDEND TAXATION

All dividends are classified into two categories: ordinary and qualified. A company earns profits in two ways. One way is through their regular operating activities, and the other is by selling their assets. The money earned from selling long-term assets is classified as capital gains. If any portion of this money is paid out to you, it's a qualified dividend. The rest of it is ordinary income.

A single dividend payment will contain portions of ordinary income as well as qualified dividends. Ordinary dividends are taxed at prevailing income tax rates. This means they're treated as an extension of the income that you earn every year. You'll pay income tax on it according to the marginal tax rate at which you usually pay income tax.

The Form 1099-DIV will list the total amount of ordinary dividends you've earned over the year. Ordinary dividends are the default mode of payment. If a company doesn't specify a category, you should assume that the money being paid is an ordinary dividend.

Qualified dividends are treated as long-term capital gains. Capital gains come in two flavors: long-term and short-term. If you were to buy a stock and sell it within a year, this is a short-term sale. Any stock that you've held for more than a year is a long-term investment. Long-term capital gains tax rates range from zero to 20%. They're lower than ordinary income tax rates, which can be as high as 37%.

The amount of capital gains tax you pay depends on your filing status and your income tax bracket. For 2020, here's what the tax rates look like (O'Shea, 2020):

Single filers

- 0 - $40,000 - Zero
- $40,001 - $441,450 - 15%
- $441,451 and above - 20%

Married filing jointly

- 0 - $80,000 - Zero
- $80,001 - $496,600 - 15%
- $496,601 and above - 20%

Head of household

- 0 - $53,600 - Zero
- $53,601 - $469,050 - 15%
- $469,051 and above - 20%

Married, filing separately

- 0 - $40,000 - Zero
- $40,001 - $248,300 - 15%
- $248,301 and above - 20%

That's all there is to dividend taxation. Depending on the category your dividend is classified under, you'll pay different tax rates. Something to note is that if you DRIP your dividends into your investment in a regular brokerage account, you'll still be liable to pay taxes. Your broker will invest the entire dividend amount into the stock or fund. At the end of the year, you'll be liable to pay taxes on those dividends. This means you'll have a cash outflow at the end of the year if you elect to DRIP. Some investors forget about DRIP taxes since they don't receive cash payments. However, you're still liable for those taxes.

The two categories mostly apply to dividends earned from stock investments. In the case of bond or bond fund investment, dividends are technically interest income, which is the same as ordinary income.

REITs

REITs are slightly more complex than stock dividends, but these complexities work in your favor. The entire issue with REIT taxation hinges on how accounting principles work. These principles are referred to as Generally Accepted Accounting Principles or GAAP. GAAP is intended to cover every single industry and company in the United States and accounts for the quirks of every one of these industries. Understandably, sometimes the rules don't make much sense.

Nowhere is this more evident than with REITs. REITs are companies that own real estate and collect rent from those properties. Consider how the average landlord handles the issue of property valuation. Over time, the value of a real estate asset rises if it's well maintained. REIT companies, therefore, own properties whose values increase as time goes by, assuming they maintain them well.

However, GAAP has a different take on how assets ought to be handled. As far as GAAP is concerned, there's no difference between an asset such as furniture and real estate. Furniture and other typical company assets depreciate over time. On a company's balance sheet, this asset's value is reduced by a fixed percentage every year, over a fixed number of years. The length of the depreciation period is referred to as the useful life period. Real estate typically has a useful life of 20 years.

This means a REIT reduces the value of its assets by a certain percentage every year. Older properties decrease in value on paper as the years go by, irrespective of their true market value. There's another issue with depreciation. It's considered an expense under GAAP and has to be subtracted from a company's revenues. This means a REIT collects rent, pays salaries and administration expenses, and further reduces their revenues by depreciating expenses. This is a non-cash expense and makes no sense for a REIT (due to the nature of their assets), but they still record it to comply with GAAP.

So what does all this have to do with dividends? Dividends are paid from the income a company produces. If REITs are decreasing their revenues through unjustified depreciation, this means REIT dividends will be greater than their recorded net income on paper. After all, depreciation isn't a cash expense. It isn't even real for the most part when it comes to a REIT (since assets are *increasing* in value). The company would rather distribute that cash than hang on to it.

This is why you'll often see payout ratios exceed 100% when it comes to REITs. Remember that the payout ratio is calculated by dividing the dividend payment by the net income. It might seem as if the REIT is paying an unsustainable dividend on the surface of it, but this isn't the case. GAAP-enforced depreciation distorts the picture. While this rule makes no sense in business terms, it makes REITs quite attractive in terms of taxation.

Here's how the IRS categorizes REIT dividends. There are two categories: ordinary dividends and Return of Capital or ROC. Ordinary dividends are treated the same way as stock dividends of the same category are; you'll pay taxes equal to your marginal income tax rate on them. However, the rub is that the IRS considers just the net income per share amount equal to ordinary dividends. The rest is ROC.

For example, let's say a REIT declared a net income on paper of $1.50 per share and paid a dividend of $2.50 per share. Here's how the dividend payment will be categorized. $1.50 (which is equal to net income) is ordinary income and $1.00 (the remainder) is ROC. From an earlier chapter on MLPs, can you recall how ROC is treated?

ROC isn't taxed immediately. Instead, it reduces the cost basis of your investment. If you bought the REIT in the preceding example for $50, your adjusted cost basis is now $49 ($50 minus $1 of ROC). The longer you hold your REIT, the less your cost basis becomes until it eventually reduces to zero. Once that happens, you'll pay long-term capital gains taxes on the ROC distribution, depending on which bracket you fall into. We've highlighted these brackets in the previous section.

If you hold onto your REIT beyond the date of your death, you'll never pay taxes on the amount by which your cost basis was reduced. In the previous example, if you keep receiving $1.00 ROC payments for 50 years, your cost basis will drop to zero. Subsequent ROC payments will attract long-term capital gains. However, the $50 worth of ROC payments that decreased your cost basis will not be taxed until you sell your investment.

Let's say you sell your REIT for $100. Your purchase price in cash was $50, but your adjusted cost basis is $0. This means the IRS will treat this as you having earned $100 in long-term capital gains from this investment. If you never sell it, you won't pay taxes. You can transfer your REIT holdings to your heirs. In this case, the IRS will record the price of the REIT on the day of your passing, and this price is now the cost basis for your heirs.

Let's say the REIT is selling for $200. The ROC clock is now officially reset to this level. Your heirs will continue to receive tax free ROC payments that will reduce their cost basis from $200, until the day they decide to sell the REIT (if at all). ROC is what makes MLPs such an attractive investment as well. If you were to invest in a REIT ETF, you can technically hold on to it forever throughout generations and earn tax-free dividend income.

Do note that this ROC method doesn't apply if you're holding REITs in a retirement account. Retirement account withdrawals are treated as ordinary income, no matter their source. The exception is in a Roth IRA where distributions are tax-free. In a traditional IRA or 401(k) you'll pay taxes on the entire principal since you contributed pre-tax dollars to those accounts.

Therefore, if you plan to hold on to a REIT indefinitely, it's best to hold it in a regular brokerage account. You will pay taxes on the ordinary dividends you receive, but as long as you don't plan on selling, the tax savings from ROC will boost your returns. If you DRIP this into your REIT, that boosts returns even further.

Like stock dividends, you don't need to do any heavy lifting when declaring taxes on the cash you receive. The REIT will indicate the amounts within the respective categories on Forms 1099-DIV and 8937. You'll simply input these numbers into your tax preparation software and pay whatever is due. If you choose to DRIP dividends, you won't see a cash distribution hit your account, so you'll need to set aside cash to pay the taxes you owe.

The 2017 Tax Cuts and Jobs Act brings two important benefits for REITs and their shareholders. Most notably, thanks to the new 20% deduction on pass-through income through the end of 2025, individual REIT shareholders can now deduct 20% of taxable REIT dividend income they receive (but not for dividends that qualify for the capital gain rates).

MLPs work in the same way, except the forms involved are different, as we previously highlighted. Generally, it's not a good idea to hold an MLP in a retirement account. This is because you'll lose the capital gains deferral advantage, as we just explained.

However, there's also another reason. MLP dividends sometimes consist of Unrelated Business Taxable Income or UBTI. If you receive UBTI greater than $1,000 in a year in a retirement account, you're in for a world of tax headaches.

You'll need to report it via a 990-T form to the IRS and pay taxes on it at your top marginal tax rate. Like the K-1, this form also arrives late and it complicates matters. The bottom line is, invest in MLPs using a regular brokerage account and not a retirement account.

We've reached the end of the taxation chapter, and you can take a deep breath now. We appreciate this might be not have been the most thrilling part of the book, but it is one of the most important. If you have any concerns, contact a tax professional, preferably one who has experience working with investors.

15

OPTIMAL PORTFOLIO CONSTRUCTION FOR DIVIDEND GROWTH INVESTING

So far, in this book, we've covered a wide variety of financial instruments you can invest in. We've also hinted at how you can construct a portfolio that will give you a good level of income. It's time to put everything together and construct a portfolio that will bring you the best results for your goals.

Anytime the subject of portfolio construction is broached, the word diversification rears its head. We are fans of diversification, but the trick is to diversify to the right degree. Diversify too much, and none of your positions will have an impact on your overall portfolio. Diversify too little, and you'll live and die by the performance of a few stocks.

There's also the matter of individual stock investing to be considered. How many positions should you own, and how should you allocate money to them? These are just some of the questions we'll be answering in this chapter. Many investors focus on picking the best instruments but neglect portfolio construction. A well-constructed portfolio minimizes risk without harming the rewards it can earn. This should be the basis on which you invest.

DIVERSIFICATION

So how should you diversify your portfolio, and is it even worth diversifying? The primary reason for diversifying is to avoid the risk of ruin. If you concentrate your money on a single investment without taking portfolio volatility into account, then you have a single point of failure. It's the same reasoning as to why we don't like investing in companies whose revenues are tied to a single product or customer. You might earn a steady 7% per year investing in AT&T, for example, but you don't want your portfolio tied to a single stock.

Before jumping into individual stocks, let's understand the reasoning behind our diversification strategies. If you're not someone who has the time to dissect a company and understand its business inside and out, then you're better off constructing a passive portfolio. This means you'll concentrate on investing in ETFs and funds. Doing this reduces your risk of losing money. The flip side is that you'll be paying management fees, and this reduces your return. This is why minimizing fees is essential and why we believe ETFs are superior to mutual funds.

A passive fund that tracks an index shouldn't charge more than 0.06% because there isn't much work that the manager needs to put into allocating capital. They simply buy and sell whatever's on the index they're tracking. This is why we often prefer Vanguard ETFs because they tend to have the lowest fees.

This isn't the case with an actively managed fund that seeks outperformance. In these cases, you'll need to evaluate the effects of fees and inflation on the returns. For example, if the fund charges you two percent in fees and earns an average return of 10% per year, your real return after considering two percent inflation is six percent.

If a passive ETF returns eight percent and charges just 0.06% in fees, you're better off investing in the ETF, despite its lower annual returns. The passive ETF will be less volatile and will increase over time since all it does is track an index. An actively managed fund will experience volatility, and you'll have to spend more time tracking its performance. Given that both investments return around the same amount after inflation, it's better to opt for the passive investment. If the active fund returns far more than the passive one, then you'd be justified in spending time monitoring it.

Fees are especially significant when you consider investing in closed-ended bond funds. Bonds as an asset class return less on an annual basis than stocks. There are exceptions like some of the funds we highlighted, but take fees into account before investing in any fund.

We recommend investing in closed-ended bond funds to boost your income. However, don't make the mistake of comparing bond fund returns to stock fund returns. For example, don't compare a bond fund that returns five percent to a stock fund that returns 10%. You need to compare apples to apples.

So how should you diversify your portfolio? To begin with, we recommend asking yourself whether you wish to invest in individual stocks. If the answer is yes, we suggest dividing your capital in proportions of 60/30/10 and allocate the majority towards managed funds, 30% towards stocks, and 10% towards alternative assets. All portions of your portfolio will have different asset allocation principles. You will need to diversify your investments in the fund portion of your portfolio.

Here is a sample asset allocation for the fund portion of your portfolio:

- Dividend ETF (35% Allocation) - Vanguard High Dividend Index (VYM) (3.15% yield)
- Treasury Bond ETF (30% Allocation) - Vanguard Treasury ETF (VGLT) (2.68% yield)
- Public REIT (15% Allocation) - Vanguard REIT Fund (VNQ) (4.53% yield)
- Closed-End Fund (10% Allocation) - Reaves Utility Income Fund (UTG) (7.43% yield)
- Master Limited Partnership (10% Allocation) - Brookfield Infrastructure (BIP) (4.64% yield)

Let's dig a little deeper into our reasoning behind this division of capital. Remember we're talking about 60% of your capital if you plan on investing in common stocks. If you don't have the time to analyze the business behind a stock, you should allocate 90% of your portfolio towards managed funds and 10% towards alternatives.

The stock ETF gives you a balance between capital gains as well a decent yield. You don't have to choose VYM, you can choose VIG instead. VIG prioritizes capital gains more than VYM does. If you're older and need to prioritize income a lot more than capital gains, we recommend choosing VYM. If you can wait for another decade or so before you need to withdraw your dividends, VIG is a better choice for you.

The treasury bond fund VGLT might seem to be a laggard in the portfolio. In fact, when times are great it will pull overall portfolio performance down. However, given that our aim is to minimize risk, VGLT should be one of the pillars of your portfolio. The point behind this position is to minimize your downside risk when markets turn bearish. Government debt is a safe haven during such times, and while VGLT will limit your gains in good times, it'll make up for it by not falling anywhere near as much or even rising during bad times.

Allocating money towards REITs is an excellent idea because you get to keep more of the dividend income you earn thanks to Return on Capital. VNQ has a lower yield than most REITs on the market, but it makes up for this with a low expense ratio and stable strategy. The fund doesn't invest in any properties but instead tracks the MSCI US Investable Market index. The objective is to capture broad-based real estate moves, instead of concentrating funds on a particular type of property that could increase your risk.

VNQ's expense ratio of 0.12% is higher than most Vanguard funds, but its port-folio is well-diversified. Industrials are the biggest proportion of its portfolio, and for this reason it suffered recently. However, VNQ is well-poised to rebound when the economy picks back up. From a risk perspective, it doesn't hold any foreign real estate, which is a good thing since there's no telling which factors will influence property values abroad.

UTG is the income-generating star in this portfolio. With a 7.4% yield, it'll generate enough income to keep you satisfied. As its name suggests, UTG is a utility fund and invests in both domestic and international utility providers. Its high dividend yield is quite safe since utility stocks tend to be stable thanks to high barrier to entry, and distribute the majority of their earnings to shareholders. They don't appreciate much in share price, which is why the high yield is necessary to compensate investors. If generating high levels of income isn't as much of a priority for you and you'd like to capture capital gains as well, consider other closed-ended funds or even allocate this portion of your portfolio to common stock.

Lastly, we have BIP, which is an MLP. BIP is an MLP of its parent firm Brook-field Asset Management (BAM), which is a prominent infrastructure investment firm. Both BAM and BIP have had a great decade, and you might be wondering which is the better stock to own. We've recommended BIP thanks to its high dividend yield.

Given the infrastructure focus of both of these companies, it's a good bet that they'll be able to withstand any recessionary pressure. BIP's high yield will also ensure that its stock price remains relatively stable. A decline in stock price will boost yield to greater levels. This will lead to more investors buying the stock and bring its yield back to its current level.

When combined with VGLT, your portfolio will withstand bearish markets quite well. Thanks to the exposure to real estate, a portion of your portfolio will move in a different cycle, which also helps mitigate risk. We had previously mentioned that 10% of your portfolio should be allocated towards alternative assets. We'll explain what alternative assets are shortly.

For now, understand that this level of diversification in your passive portfolio is ideal. You have investments in every asset class and aren't overly exposed to risk. Your portfolio is U.S.-concentrated, which is a very good thing. Despite its current troubles, the American economic system will stay strong in the near term. You might be tempted to buy Chinese tech stock ETFs, but consider the risk before doing so. It's hard enough to figure out what's happening in the American market, let alone trying to figure out how a government-manipulated stock market like the Chinese one will work.

Let's move on and take a look at the common stock portion of your portfolio. Remember that if you don't wish to invest in common stocks, you'll split your money in a 90/10 split between funds and alternatives.

If you have the time to evaluate individual businesses, you should split your money in a 60/30/10 split between funds, common stock, and alternatives.

Portfolio Concentration

When investing in common stock, your objective is outperformance. If you review the investment principles we outlined earlier in this book, you'll realize that every principle is intended to keep you invested in a great business that keeps delivering capital gains as well as dividends. The lower the dividends you get paid, the higher your capital gains will be.

If you're going to invest directly into a stock, it doesn't make sense to over diversify. This is a controversial statement and flies against most financial advice. However, it's what investors such as Warren Buffett, Charlie Munger, and Mark Cuban prescribe.

To understand why, you need to look at your investment in a company from a business perspective. Let's say you're really good at something and start a company. Once the company starts doing well, would it make sense to divide your time between your company and a full-time job? Would such diversification make sense?

We don't think so. If your skill is good enough to get you paid lots of money, you're better off investing time into developing that skill instead of taking time away from it and working a "stable" job just for the sake of diversification. Allocating money in your portfolio towards common stocks works the same way. If you're convinced that a business is excellent and that it has great prospects, you should buy as much of it as possible.

As long as you can buy it at a reasonable price, you should be buying all the time. If you have $1,000 and have spotted two companies that are selling for prices that are bargains, how should you proceed? There's no template in such a scenario. You can buy more of the company that is giving you the best bargain. Or you could split your cash between both companies. The prices you can buy those company shares at are what matter the most. As long as the business conditions remain the same and as long as the price you receive is fair, you should be buying.

Doing this will result in a concentrated portfolio. You'll be buying many great businesses without worrying about holding 50+ different stocks. For example, Charlie Munger holds just three positions in his personal portfolio. He understands all three businesses in there and doesn't bother adding more in the name of diversification. By investing in what he knows and by following his principles, he reduces his risk considerably. If you are new to investing, we generally recommend you stick to less than 20 individual stocks in your first 2-3 years.

Portfolio concentration will bring you massive gains when your businesses do well. However, it'll also sink or swim based on the fortunes of the companies you invest in. Many investors get scared away by this volatility and consider concentration a bad thing. We'd like to point out that there are many caveats you need to satisfy before you decide to concentrate your money into a few holdings.

First, you need to have enough time to be able to evaluate a business thoroughly. This doesn't need to be a full-time job, but you need to dedicate at least 30 minutes a day. Second, you need to follow the investment principles we've outlined in this book. Not only do you need to follow them, but you also have to understand why they're effective. Many investors think they understand successful investing principles. Still, when it comes to buying companies, they let their emotions get in the way and end up doing the exact opposite.

Lastly, it would be best if you got your stable passive portfolio in place before investing actively. This will ensure you'll have some degree of stability at all times. As Warren Buffett famously said

> *"There are two rules in investing.*
> *Rule No. 1: Never lose money.*
> *Rule No. 2: Never forget rule No. 1."*

ALTERNATIVE ASSETS

Alternative assets refer to investments that don't always have a business tied to them. For example, a common stock or bond is attached to a business. Whereas alternative assets such as gold or silver are not businesses. Instead, their prices are driven by their individual economic cycles and the state of the global economy.

Many investors consider them speculative since most alternatives don't have any value beyond what someone else thinks they're worth. However, we contend that alternative assets have a place in everyone's portfolio, albeit in the right proportions.

Let's take a look at some alternative assets and how you should invest in them.

Precious Metals

Gold, silver, platinum, palladium, etc. fall under the precious metals category. The most famous precious metals are gold and silver, of course. Gold is an excellent example of an alternative asset that is speculative but still contains a lot of value. Gold doesn't have any value beyond what someone else thinks it's worth. However, human beings have attributed monetary value to gold for more than 5,000 years, which is why it's considered precious.

If everyone were to decide tomorrow that gold isn't all that attractive, then it wouldn't be worth anything. This hasn't happened, and as a result, gold has always played an important part in the global economy. Traditionally, it's viewed as a safe haven asset. People have always valued gold, and there's no doubt that if paper money were to get devalued, gold would still be a viable currency. This is why gold rises in value whenever the values of the dollar and other major currencies decline.

Gold is a particularly viable investment these days because of the money printing policies that are in place in the developed world. As the amount of cash in a system increases, inflation rises, and with it, the value of money drops. Therefore gold is currently viewed as a great hedge against a falling dollar. Which is why its value has risen steadily since 2011, when Quantitative Easing really started ramping up.

Silver closely tracks gold, but it isn't quite the same. Silver has industrial uses, and there is more of a supply and demand component to its prices. Over the long run, silver tracks gold's movements despite being much cheaper than gold. It's also viewed as a desirable currency, and this adds a speculative element to its price.

The main difference is that silver doesn't function fully as a hedge against a declining dollar. Investing in it isn't as straightforward as gold, thanks to the industrial element present.

The other precious metals don't receive too much attention from retail investors, and even institutional investors who operate in them are highly specialized. As a result, we don't recommend investing into them. Gold and silver are great choices and even if you restrict yourself to gold, that's more than enough.

You can add Gold to your portfolio in many ways. You can buy the metal in physical form, or you can invest in an ETF that tracks its price. You can also invest in an ETF that tracks the fortunes of companies whose businesses are closely tied to gold.

Our favorite way to get gold exposure is slightly different, though. You can purchase companies like Royal Gold Inc. (RGLD) (1.19% yield) or Franco-Nevada Corp (FNV) (1.41% yield). Both of these companies are gold streamers.

Streaming is a great business that gives you exposure to the profits of individual companies without exposing yourself to price movements in gold.

Here's how it works. Mining companies are cash-dependent and have huge capital expenses. They routinely seek out loans and financing to fund their operations. Mining is also a risky business. If the mine doesn't produce the projected output of metal, companies face huge losses. Bank interest rates tend to be high for gold miners, and this is where miners turn to streaming companies. A streaming company provides miners with financing, but instead of charging interest, they buy metal yielded from the mine at a steep discount. The streamer then sells the metal back to the market at regular prices and earns a profit.

The risk in streaming is that the company is exposed to mine risk. This is why it's important to invest in streaming companies that know what they're doing and evaluate mines thoroughly. The companies we've highlighted produce not only capital gains but also pay steady dividends. This makes them good bets for an income-driven investor.

The most important thing to remember is that not all exposures to gold are created equal. To highlight this further, here are the returns for four different gold entities over the past ten years.

- Franco Nevada (streamer): 197.18%
- Physical Gold price: 37.97%
- Gold ETF (GLD): 32.62%
- Barrick Gold (miner): -47.27%

Even though physical gold rose in price, mining companies like Barrick Gold suffered, while streamers such as Franco Nevada outperformed the metal itself.

Oil

After gold, oil is the most talked about commodity. Oil prices influence entire economies, and wars are fought over it. However, it's a bad idea to invest money with an aim of profiting from its price moves through ETFs or futures.

This isn't because of the rise of alternative energy sources. Oil is a poor investment because it has its own supply and demand element, along with a liberal dose of speculation. The price of oil often fluctuates based on what some kingdom in the Middle East decides to do and how American demand fluctuates.

Retail investors are best served staying away from oil. Even ETFs and companies tied to oil aren't a good bet because their incomes aren't stable. It takes companies the size of Chevron and Exxon, with deep resources and multiple income streams derived from oil, to generate steady income.

Agricultural Commodities

Agricultural commodities are an obscure class of alternatives as far as retail investors go. They aren't easily traded, and despite there being a few ETFs around, they don't garner much attention. Corn and soybeans are the two most heavily traded commodities in this asset class. Their prices usually track one another.

Given that they're crops, their output heavily depends on weather patterns and conditions. To invest in them successfully, you'll need to understand how supply and demand work in this sector. Institutions that support them are highly specialized and typically don't invest in anything else. Therefore, individual investors should stay away from commodities.

Other Alternatives

There are an increasing number of alternative assets that pay dividends. Cryptocurrencies are a popular alternative asset, but they don't pay dividends. However, we believe dedicating a small portion of your portfolio (5-10%) to Bitcoin is worth it as a hedge against the broad stock market. We will be covering Bitcoin in greater depth in our next book *The Only Bitcoin Investing Book You'll Ever Need*, which is scheduled for release in late February 2021.

Artwork, wine, jewelry, and classic cars are good places to park your money. However, these are mostly one-off purchases, and as such, we won't spend time discussing them since it's hard to develop a repeatable and consistent system. If you have a significant advantage in this area, then, by all means, go ahead.

Shipping containers have become more popular of late, with some companies advertising 25% returns per year. In our experience, most of these companies are flat-out frauds so it's best to stay away from this field entirely.

When it comes to alternative assets, stick with gold. Then add some Bitcoin in as a hedge. Most importantly, don't overcomplicate things.

Remember that your primary aim with alternative assets is to create your own personal financial fortress, not spend time learning the ins and outs of various obscure asset classes.

FREEMAN INCOME INVESTING RULE #9

HAVING 5% OF YOUR PORTFOLIO IN BITCOIN IS A GREAT HEDGE AGAINST A BROAD MARKET COLLAPSE

CONCLUSION

If you're looking for income from your investments, then the dividend growth strategy is your best bet. We hope this book has opened your eyes to the benefits of this approach.

It's important for you to remain realistic when seeking income from your investments. First things first, look at minimizing costs wherever possible. If your financial advisor is charging 1-2% to tell you to invest in a mutual fund that also charges 1% per year, you already need to make an extra 2% per year just to cover your fees.

Remember that with the rise in passive ETFs, you no longer have to pay 1-2% for a broad market fund, and can pay as little as 0.03% per year. By simply switching from a mutual fund to a passive ETF, your savings compound to a significant amount over the course of 10-20 years.

By concentrating on stability and avoiding yield chasing, you'll avoid most of the income investing traps out there. Stay focused on minimizing risk as much as possible, and this won't be an issue for you.

Remember that capital gains are just as crucial as dividends are. Without steady capital gains, you'll end up losing your investment principal, and your dividend income will inevitably decline because of it, if the company slashes its payouts. These days, low interest rates have created a ton of dividend and yield traps, so watch out for these stocks. Don't automatically assume a high yield is a good thing.

What truly matters is a stock's payout ratio and a history of growing dividend payments. A sustainable payout ratio varies from one industry to another. But as long as the dividend payment is growing and the payout ratio remains stable, you'll end up earning more income as time goes by. This is the essence of income investing, and it's what you should aim for. Don't chase monthly dividend payments for their own sake. A monthly payment that yields five percent is no different from a semi-yearly payment that yields the same amount.

We've provided you with a set of investment options within the managed fund sphere, but if you wish to invest in individual companies, you need to follow a repeatable investment process. We've outlined the 11 principles in our approach. These principles will help you unearth great companies that pay steady dividends and will grow over time. The most important thing to look for is a quality business. Everything else comes second.

Constructing a portfolio can seem overwhelming at first, but we're positive that you've gained some insight into how you should approach it and will find a simplified 60/30/10 approach practical. You can build a diversified portfolio or one that has elements of diversification and concentration within it. A concentrated portfolio is best when investing in individual companies. Keep in mind that there are a few caveats you need to satisfy before you decide to concentrate your holdings into a few stocks. Above all else, you need to follow the sound investment principles we've elaborated on in this book.

Feel free to use our recommended stocks such as AT&T, ExxonMobil, and Realty Income as a starting point for more research or as parts of your portfolio. For further research, we recommend examining the latest 10-K reports from each company, as well as checking key financial metrics using our *Company Valuation 101* criteria, which you can access for free at https://freemanpublications.com/bonus

Investing for income is critical as you grow older, but it doesn't have to be complicated. Make it a point to refer to this book whenever you have any doubts.

Alternatively, you can email us at admin@freemanpublications.com if you would like something clarified. We answer every single reader email.

2020 was a chaotic year, so as we move into 2021, we wish you the best of luck with your investing!

One final word from us. If this book has helped you in any way, we'd appreciate it if you left a review on Amazon.

Reviews are the lifeblood of our business. We read every single one and incorporate your feedback into our future book projects.

To leave an Amazon review, go to

https://freemanpublications.com/leaveareview

"THE MOST SUCCESSFUL PEOPLE IN LIFE ARE THE ONES WHO ASK QUESTIONS. THEY'RE ALWAYS LEARNING. THEY'RE ALWAYS GROWING. THEY'RE ALWAYS PUSHING."

- *Robert Kiyosaki*

CONTINUING YOUR JOURNEY

Like Robert Kiyosaki said on the previous page, "The most successful people in life are always learning, growing, and asking questions."

Which is why we created our investing community, aptly named *How To NOT Lose Money in the Stock Market,* so that like-minded individuals could get together to share ideas and learn from each other.

We regularly run giveaways, share wins from our readers, and you'll be the first to know when our new books are released.

It's 100% free, and there are no requirements to join, except for the willingness to learn.

You can join us on Facebook by going to

http://freemanpublications.com/facebook

ACKNOWLEDGMENTS

This book is a team effort, and while I get to be the face of the business and receive all the kind messages from readers, I can't ignore the people who helped make this book what it was.

Thank you first to our content team for their writing, editing, and proofreading efforts and dealing with my persistent questions about why specific changes needed to be made.

Thank you to Mark Greenberg, our superstar narrator, who has really become "the voice" of Freeman Publications over the past year.

Thank you to Ed Fahy over at UBF for always being there every time I needed to make a minor update to the book interior.

Thank you to all 52 Freeman readers who participated in our advanced reader program for this book. Your notes and feedback were invaluable in going from the final draft to the finished product. I'd particularly like to highlight the efforts of Jakub Wierzba, Stevie Christie and Yacoob Kathrada.

A special mention must go to David Buck for his incredibly detailed feedback ranging from things we didn't clarify well enough to points we outright missed.

Without your input, this book simply would not have been as good as it is today, so for that David, I thank you.

Thank you to everyone who picked up the phone when I called to ask if they were free for 5 minutes, only to spend an hour discussing the merits of one company versus another. You know who you are.

Thank you to our hundreds of readers on social media for your words of encouragement throughout this project.

Finally, thank you to my family, whose initial uncertainty of "are you still doing that book thing" has blossomed into full support for my vision here at Freeman Publications. This means more than you will ever know.

Oliver
London, England
January, 2021

OTHER BOOKS BY FREEMAN
PUBLICATIONS (AVAILABLE ON AMAZON
& AUDIBLE)

The 8-Step Beginner's Guide to
Value Investing: Featuring 20 for 20
- The 20 Best Stocks & ETFs to Buy
and Hold for The Next 20 Years

Bear Market Investing Strategies: 37
Recession-Proof Ideas to Grow Your
Wealth - Including Inverse ETFs, Put
Options, Gold & Cryptocurrency

Iron Condor Options for Beginners: A
Smart, Safe Method to Generate an
Extra 25% Per Year with Just 2
Trades Per Month

COVERED
CALLS
—— *for* ——
BEGINNERS

A RISK-FREE WAY TO COLLECT
RENTAL INCOME" EVERY SINGLE MONTH ON
STOCKS YOU ALREADY OWN

FREEMAN PUBLICATIONS

<u>Covered Calls for Beginners: A Risk-Free Way to Collect "Rental Income" Every Single Month on Stocks You Already Own</u>

CREDIT
SPREAD
OPTIONS
—— *for* ——
BEGINNERS

TURN YOUR MOST BORING STOCKS INTO
RELIABLE MONTHLY PAYCHECKS
—— *using* ——
CALL, PUT & IRON BUTTERFLY SPREADS
EVEN IF THE MARKET IS DOING NOTHING.

FREEMAN PUBLICATIONS

<u>Credit Spread Options for Beginners: Turn Your Most Boring Stocks into Reliable Monthly Paychecks using Call, Put & Iron Butterfly Spreads - Even If The Market is Doing Nothing</u>

REFERENCES

2Q20 Earnings Conference Call Edited Transcript. (2020). Chevron. https://chevroncorp.gcs-web.com/static-files/10f71f7d-4347-40af-a329-baef3615e2bf

2015 Letter - Klarman tell investors he is looking for bargains amid "stealth bear market." (2020, November 4). 2015 Letter - Klarman Tell Investors He Is Looking for Bargains amid "Stealth Bear Market." https://valuewalkposts.tumblr.com/post/138102275370/2015-letter-klarman-tell-investors-he-is

Bengen, W. (2020). *DETERMINING WITHDRAWAL RATES USING HISTORICAL DATA.* https://www.retailinvestor.org/pdf/Bengen1.pdf

Chen, J. (2020, November 4). *K-Shaped Recovery Definition.* Investopedia. https://www.investopedia.com/k-shaped-recovery-5080086

de Haas, B. (2020, October 13). *Why Dan Loeb Wants Disney To Cease Its Dividend.* https://seekingalpha.com/article/4378797-why-dan-loeb-wants-disney-to-cease-dividend

Facebook's advertising revenue worldwide from 2009 to 2019 (2020). Statista https://www.statista.com/statistics/271258/facebooks-advertising-revenue-worldwide/

Finke, M. (2020, November 4). *Are Nontraded REITs Right for Clients?* ThinkAdvisor. https://www.thinkadvisor.com/2014/11/24/are-nontraded-reits-right-for-clients/

Foelber, D. (2020, July 29). *Is Kinder Morgan Stock a Buy?* The Motley Fool. https://www.fool.com/investing/2020/07/29/is-kinder-morgan-stock-a-buy.aspx

Frankel, M. (2020, November 4). *Pros and Cons of Single-Tenant Net Leases for Investors.* Millionacres. https://www.fool.com/millionacres/real-estate-investing/articles/pros-and-cons-single-tenant-net-leases-investors

Graham, B., & Dodd, D. L. (2009). *Security analysis: principles and technique.* Mcgraw-Hill.

Hedge Funds: Higher Returns Or Just High Fees? (2019). Investopedia. https://www.investopedia.com/articles/03/121003.asp

Here's How Much Warren Buffett Has Made on Coca-Cola. (2019, November 19). Nasdaq.Com. https://www.nasdaq.com/articles/heres-how-much-warren-buffett-has-made-on-coca-cola-2019-11-19

Is Tesla Losing Money on Every Car Sale? (2019). Investopedia. https://www.investopedia.com/articles/markets/070116/tesla-losing-money-each-time-it-sells-car-tsla.asp

Japan's Expansionist Policies Have Brought Unexpected Results. (2019). Investopedia. https://www.investopedia.com/articles/markets/052516/japans-case-study-diminished-effects-qe.asp

Lynch, P., & Rothchild, J. (2000). *One up on Wall Street.* Simon & Schuster.

Maverick, J. B. (2019). *What is the average annual return for the S&P 500?* Investopedia. https://www.investopedia.com/ask/answers/042415/what-average-annual-return-sp-500.asp

McClay, R. (2020, November 4). *The Benefits of Master Limited Partnerships.* Investopedia. https://www.investopedia.com/investing/benefits-master-limited-partnerships/

Medical Cannabis Market – Global Industry Trends And Forecast To 2027 (2020). | Data Bridge Market Research. https://www.databridgemarketresearch.com/reports/global-medical-cannabis-market

Nikola: How to Parlay An Ocean of Lies Into a Partnership With the Largest Auto OEM in America. (2020, September 10). Hindenburg Research. https://hindenburgresearch.com/nikola/

O'Shea, A. (2020, November 4). *2020 Capital Gains Tax Rates & How to Avoid a Big Bill.* NerdWallet. https://www.nerdwallet.com/article/taxes/capital-gains-tax-rates

Pisani, B. (2019, March 15). *Active fund managers trail the S&P 500 for the ninth year in a row in triumph for indexing.* CNBC; CNBC. https://www.cnbc.com/2019/03/15/active-fund-managers-trail-the-sp-500-for-the-ninth-year-in-a-row-in-triumph-for-indexing.html

Realty Income Announces Operating Results For Second Quarter And First Six Months Of 2020. (2020, November 4). Www.Realtyincome.Com. https://www.realtyincome.com/investors/press-releases/press-release-details/2020/Realty-Income-Announces-Operating-Results-For-Second-Quarter-And-First-Six-Months-Of-2020/default.aspx

Shah, A. (2020, November 4). *Obscure Berkshire Hathaway Filing Reveals What Warren Buffett Thinks About Kraft Heinz.* Forbes. https://www.forbes.com/sites/alapshah/2019/08/12/obscure-berkshire-hathaway-filing-reveals-what-warren-buffett-thinks-about-kraft-heinz/#7947aaec3b82

Sparks, D. (2020, January 15). *Battle of Dividends: Apple vs. Microsoft.* The Motley Fool. https://www.fool.com/investing/2020/01/15/battle-of-dividends-apple-vs-microsoft.aspx

Trade Signals - FANG Stocks Up 400%, S&P 500 Index ex-FANGs up 35%, S&P 500 Index up 45% (2015-Present). (2020, November 4). CMG. https://www.cmgwealth.com/ri/trade-signals-fang-stocks-up-400-sp-500-index-ex-fangs-up-35-sp-500-index-up-45-2015-present/

US dividends for the long term. (2013). JP Morgan.

What to know about buying closed-end funds at a discount. (2020, November 4). Nuveen. https://www.nuveen.com/en-us/thinking/closed-end-funds/what-to-know-about-buying-closed-end-funds-at-a-discount

Why the Fed saved AIG and not Lehman. (2020, November 4). Fortune. https://fortune.com/2010/09/02/why-the-fed-saved-aig-and-not-lehman/

Williams, D. (2020, November 4). *Where Does The U.S. Housing Market Go From Here? Five Experts Share Predictions For The Rest Of 2020.* Forbes. https://www.forbes.com/sites/dimawilliams/2020/07/10/is-it-going-to-get-better-before-it-gets-worse-five-experts-share-predictions-for-the-us-housing-market-in-the-second-half-of-2020/#6730e1a07026

Williams, S. (2020, July 24). *The 4 Biggest Dividend Payouts on Wall Street.* The Motley Fool. https://www.fool.com/investing/2020/07/24/the-4-biggest-dividend-payouts-on-wall-street.aspx

Winck, B. (2020, April 24). *Nintendo cuts 'Animal Crossing: New Horizons' interest rates to boost virtual spending.* Business Insider. https://markets.businessinsider.com/news/stocks/nintendo-cuts-interest-rate-animal-crossing-new-horizons-stimulate-spending-2020-4-1029127954#:~:

Printed in the USA
CPSIA information can be obtained
at www.ICGtesting.com
LVHW041257170424
777534LV00009B/918

9 781838 267360